For Dot

When
Women
Walk
Alone

Let the Lord draw you closer during this season of your life—He is your "Husband," new (Isaiah 54)

CINDI McMENAMIN

Cindi McMenamin

HARVEST HOUSE PUBLISHERS
EUGENE, OREGON

Cover by Koechel Peterson & Associates, Inc., Minneapolis, Minnesota

Cover photo © James Thew / Shutterstock

Some of the names have been changed to protect the anonymity and privacy of the women who shared their stories in this book.

WHEN WOMEN WALK ALONE
Copyright © 2002, 2012 by Cindi McMenamin
Published by Harvest House Publishers
Eugene, Oregon 97402
www.harvesthousepublishers.com

ISBN 978-0-7369-4822-7 (pbk.)
ISBN 978-0-7369-4823-4 (eBook)

The Library of Congress has cataloged the edition as follows:
  McMenamin, Cindi, 1965-
  When Women Walk Alone / Cindi McMenamin
    p. cm.
  ISBN-13: 978-0-7369-0743-9
    1. Christian women—Religious life. 2. Solitude—Religious aspects—Christianity.
  3. Loneliness—Religious aspects—Christianity. I. Title.
  BV4527 .M433 2002
  248.8'43—dc 21

Printed in the United States of America

16 17 18 19 20 / BP-CD / 10 9 8 7 6

For women—everywhere—who feel they walk alone...

Acknowledgments

My heartfelt thanks to the women who have read this book, brought it to their churches and started study groups with it, and purchased it for the women in their family—or in some cases, every woman they know! This revised and updated version would not be possible if you hadn't picked up this book, gleaned from it, and passed it on. Thank you for caring about women who walk alone.

Contents

A Personal Note from Cindi 7

A Cry from the Desert 11

Part One—A Season of Searching

1. Alone as a Woman: Seeking the Blessing. 19
2. Alone at Heart: Looking to Your Heavenly
   Husband. 31
3. Alone as a Parent: Partnering with God. 47

Part Two—A Season of Strengthening

4. Alone in Your Pain: Releasing the Burden 63
5. Alone in Your Spiritual Life: Developing a
   Deeper Trust. 79
6. Alone in Worship: Experiencing More of God 99
7. Alone in Your Trials: Finding Your Glory Story 117

Part Three—A Season of Soaring

8. Alone in Your Restlessness: Becoming Desperate
   for God. 137
9. Alone in Your Dreams: Knowing God Is
   for You 155
10. Alone in Serving: Relating to the Heart of Jesus 171
11. Alone with Your God: Living in His
    Abundance. 191

Welcome to the Oasis 209

Appendix: Surrendering the Struggle 211

Small Group Leader's Guide 213

Notes 227

A Personal Note from Cindi

❦

In the Spring of 2001, I lay face-down on the floor of my study and prayed, "God, I can't write this book. I have no idea how to touch the hearts of hurting women. I need *You* to help me."

I was convinced it was the book God wanted me to write. After all, the title came to me so clearly as I rode a train from Southern to Central California just months earlier and prayed for direction for my second book. "Who do I write for next, God? What is the burden on *Your* heart?"

His answer was one I heard only in the deep recesses of my heart: *When women walk alone.*

Yet several months later, as I faced a deadline to finish the book, I cried out to God for help. And in that moment of brokenness I realized I didn't have what it took to write for that kind of burden on God's heart. Yes, I've experienced what I feel is loneliness—as a woman, as a wife, as a mother. But I have not walked through the depths of despair that many women have walked—the loss of a husband through death or divorce, the devastating loss of a child, the dark void of depression, the agony of aloneness that comes from an illness or disability or dashed dreams or never having married. I have not faced what some desperate hearts will have experienced as they pick up this book. "God help me," I prayed. "You know who will read this and what it is they will need to read to experience healing and hope. Bring me the women with encouragement to share. Bring me the stories that will change lives."

Three months later, I turned in the manuscript for the book that has now sold more than 100,000 copies. Thousands of women have shared with me through letters, emails, and in person how their lives were transformed through the stories in this book of women who grew through their grief—stories that testify of the truly incredible ways God can work in people's lives.

From single women out on the mission field...

    to widows dealing with the loss of their husbands of 30 years or more.

From wives in loveless marriages...

    to women who wonder if they'll ever be married.

From those who feel they've fallen too far for God's grace...

    to those in ministry who feel alone and misunderstood.

From career women who feel alone at the top...

    to stay-at-home moms struggling with a sense of purpose.

I've heard from them all. I've heard their stories of hope as they discovered, through the pages of this book, that there is a reason for their aloneness, and there is One who is strengthening them through it.

One particularly memorable story is that of a woman named Angelique, whom I met while speaking at a women's retreat. Angelique, a single mother of a then nine-year-old, was in her one-bedroom apartment ready to take her life when she heard a knock on her door. When she opened it, there stood two women from her church. They handed her this book and said, "We thought of you this evening while we were in a group study on this book. We wanted you to have this. And we'd love for you to join us next week."

As they left, Angelique opened the book and by the time she got to the end of the first chapter, she was on her knees at the edge of her bed, tears flowing down her face.

"It never ever occurred to me that there might be a reason for the pain I've had in my life," she told me at the retreat. "When I realized God wanted to draw me closer to Him through my aloneness, it changed my life and made me want to live again."

Instead of taking her life that night, Angelique gave it to Jesus. And the next week she showed up at the small group study at her church and shared her story of giving life—and Jesus—a chance. The women in her study pitched in financially to give Angelique a scholarship to attend the upcoming women's retreat, and that made it possible for her to share with me how the book had changed her life.

There may be other Angeliques out there who have yet to discover there *is* a reason and a purpose behind their pain. And if you're one of them, I invite you to discover one of the most amazing and life-changing truths there is—the God of the Universe wants to develop an intimate relationship with you. And if He has to lead you out to a desert of aloneness to do it, that's what He'll do, so He can show you who He is and all that He can accomplish in your life.

The power in this book is not my own. It's a power that comes from the truth of who God is and the power of His Word—which can cut to the core of our hearts and transform lives. You'll read about women of the Bible and women of today who encountered God and His truth in their season of aloneness, and came through it changed. Changed, strengthened, and hopeful again.

May you become another one of the real-life stories of a woman changed by her encounter with God in the desert of aloneness. And may you, too, discover more intimately the One who has been waiting to get alone with *you*.

Walking alongside you,
Cindi McMenamin
Southern California
2012

A Cry from the Desert

❧

ouldn't it be nice to never again have to feel alone? Imagine, instead, someone beside you whenever you needed to sense your worth as a woman, a shoulder available whenever you needed to cry, strong arms holding you up as you pursued your dream. Think of what it would be like to always sense the strength and wisdom of another who has gone before you in the seasons of life and can help you through the ones that seem to overwhelm you.

Yet as women, we so often feel like we walk through life alone. Sometimes certain situations in life cause us to feel alone, like when a husband walks out of (or never walked into) your life, when a child leaves home, a parent dies, or a friend moves away. Sometimes we feel alone during specific seasons of our life—when we deal with marital tensions or the stress of being single, when we parent young children or find we can't have children, when we reach the afternoon of life and our children leave home, when our body slows down, and when we retire from our jobs. Sometimes just the stress and pace of life makes us feel we walk alone... thinking no one understands our plans or hears our hearts or has walked in our pumps.

If that's how *you* feel, you are *not* alone. Not only are you surrounded by other women who feel the same way, you're also surrounded by shoulders that *can* carry your burdens, strong arms that *do* hold you up, and strength and wisdom that *wants* to be part of your life. This book aims at opening your eyes to see all that you have—and to convince you that you can be stronger than you've ever been before by embracing the One who has perhaps led you to your desert of aloneness to show you a mightier side of Himself.

In this book, I want to look at what we as women consider "alone times" and help you see them as doorways to discovering a deeper intimacy with God. I want to help you walk from the desert of aloneness to the oasis of abundance by seeing your alone times not as obstacles to your growth, but as opportunities to draw closer to the heart of God.

I believe that God often draws us out to the desert where we're feeling alone to show us a side of Himself we might not otherwise see if we were in an arena of abundance. Consider for a moment, a few stories in the Bible of women who were alone in the desert and had a life-changing encounter with the living God:

- Hagar—the Egyptian maid of Abraham's wife, Sarah— was single, pregnant, and running from home when she lay down by a desert well and prepared to die. No one understood her plight. No one cared, she thought. But rather than meeting death in the desert sun that day, she met the Giver of Life, who gave her enough strength to return home, bear her child, and live the rest of her days resting in God's promises. Had Hagar been comforted by a man or a well-meaning friend in her distress, she would've missed her amazing encounter with "the God who sees" (Genesis 16:13).

- Leah, a woman who was given to her husband Jacob out of trickery, found herself feeling desperate and alone in a loveless marriage to a man who really loved her sister, Rachel. After bearing several children, feeling that would draw her husband's heart toward her, she finally learned to stop looking to the man whose love she could

never win and instead started living for the One who had
always loved her. Had Leah felt loved and fulfilled by
Jacob, she might never have discovered—in the desert of
her marriage—the Lord God as her "spiritual husband"
(Genesis 29:16-35).

- A Samaritan woman who had found her security in the
  men in her life (five previous husbands, and then a live-
  in boyfriend) found herself alone at a well, feeling empty
  and dry, when she met Jesus, who offered her a new life
  and a fulfillment she couldn't get anywhere else. Had
  she been in a place of abundance, she never would have
  found her "Living Water" (John 4:5-26).

Can you see a pattern emerging? In all three of these situations—
Hagar by the desert well, Leah in the desert of her marriage, and the
Samaritan woman by the desert road—there was water of refreshment close by. Each of these women came to the desert dried out and
empty, and they all found their oasis of strength and their living water
in their life-changing encounter with God.

If you're like Hagar—feeling mistreated or misunderstood—you,
too, may be on the verge of encountering "the God who sees." If
you're like Leah, feeling alone and neglected in your marriage, you
may be about to experience God as your "spiritual husband." Or, if
you're like the Samaritan woman, feeling alone in your desert—even
with a man in your life—you may be about to discover that your "Living Water" is just around the corner. We'll meet other women of the
Bible as well in this book—women who were feeling alone physically,
emotionally, and spiritually. And from them, we'll discover what we
can do when we walk alone—how we can find the Oasis of Satisfac-
tion from which to drink, an Abundance of Comfort to which we
can run, and a Listener with whom we can talk.

As you walk with me through this book, I hope to not only show
you the oasis that awaits you in your current desert of aloneness, but
also prepare you for the seasons of aloneness that may lie ahead. After

all, as we go through life—and grapple with singlehood or marriage, motherhood or childlessness, career or restlessness, aging and illness, menopause, retirement, and the loss of loved ones—there will constantly be new deserts of aloneness to walk through. We will not be learning how to avoid these seasons of loneliness, but rather, we will learn how we can strengthen ourselves in order to be ready when that path unfolds before us.

During my early 20s, I faced a choice as to whether I would die in my desert of aloneness or bloom in it. I had just come out of a four-year relationship with a man I thought I would marry. Overwhelmed with the feeling that I might be alone forever, I clung to God and learned to depend on His presence, His love, and His comfort during the alone times. Because He was there, filling that void in my life for *someone,* I became quite an independent woman—independent of another person, but *totally dependent* on God.

Then God brought a wonderful man into my life. But in the early years of our marriage, I began shifting my focus from dependence on God to dependence on the love and companionship of my husband. Eventually, I found myself lonely in love…and feeling desperate in the desert again. The loneliness spilled into other areas and eventually became a consuming force in my life until I realized why it was there in the first place.

As I returned to that dependence on God and saw Him begin to fill the hunger in my heart, I gained a new strength to stand alone. And in doing so, I learned some practical ways to grow stronger during the alone times that blow in and out of my life.

Today, the alone times still come:

- When I don't feel emotionally connected to those close to me.
- When I venture into something unfamiliar and don't feel I have support or encouragement.
- When I'm busy and feel I've lost touch with my friends.

- When I'm stressed out and people don't understand the pace of my life.

- When I lose someone I love through death, distance, or circumstances beyond my control.

- When I'm deluded by a crisis and don't feel the help or support of others.

My first reaction to feelings of aloneness is to struggle with them. But when I see them as invitations to be alone with God, and see another side of Him, I experience new strength, new peace, and new growth, spiritually, as God goes to work filling that hollow in my heart and making me stronger from the inside out.

Do you, too, want to be stronger, no matter what life throws you? Do you want to climb out of *your* loneliness pit and grow, rather than grieve, through your alone times? Do you want to eventually *long* for aloneness...not the kind that leaves you aching inside and feeling powerless, but the kind that strengthens you by drawing you to the side of the One who loves you more than you can fathom?

Then come with me on this journey as we look at practical ways to grow stronger through the seasons of our lives. We'll look at being alone as a woman, a wife, and a mother, and how those seasons of searching lead us to see another side of God. We'll look at being alone in our pain, alone in our spiritual life, alone in worship, and alone in our trials, and how our struggles can actually be seasons of strengthening. And finally, we'll look at being alone in our restlessness, alone in pursuing our dreams, and alone with our God, and how those times can lead us to a season of soaring to new heights with renewed strength.

Now, I realize that as you read through the stories and situations I'll present, you'll find that not all of the "deserts" will relate to your particular situation. But I encourage you to read those portions of the book anyway so you'll know how to encourage and offer hope to other women who may be walking that path.

As we embark on this journey, I trust you will find strength to not only stand ready, walk steady, and run swiftly through the seasons of your life, but also to lift up other women who may be lying alongside the road, weakened by the weariness of walking alone.

So, are you ready? Come with me—let's take a look at those painful times alone and see them as precious times we can grow. Let's walk together through those phases and stages of life that no one else seems to understand and find that helping hand that is extended toward us. Let's gain strength during our moments or miles of solitude and become all God intends for us to be.

It's been said that the true test of a woman's strength is how strong she is alone. So, let's gain strength together, my friend, and together, become stronger alone.

PART ONE

A Season of Searching

*"You will seek Me and find Me when you
search for Me with all your heart."*

—JEREMIAH 29:13 NASB

Alone as a Woman:

SEEKING THE BLESSING

*J*ulia remembers those agonizing years of walking alone.

She was young, married to a good man, and had four small children. And she was doing all she could to be a good wife and mother. But having to move every year to a new home, new church, and new area of the country for her husband's schooling was beginning to take its toll on her. Once she and her family settled into a new home, her husband would be gone 10-12 hours a day, studying and commuting to and from the university. Being shy and withdrawn, Julia didn't make friends easily, and she eventually quit trying to connect with *anyone,* figuring she'd never be in one place long enough to develop a relationship. Feeling inundated with loneliness and despair, and feeling trapped in her home during long winter months when she had no car and there was a foot of snow outside her home, Julia spiraled downward into a pit of depression, immersing herself in soap operas and television game shows as her only form of adult stimulation.

When Julia's husband graduated from school, her hopes that life would get better soon diminished. Her husband took a job that required traveling about 25 days out of every month, leaving her to live like a single parent. Then he admitted to her he didn't love her anymore and wanted out of the marriage. But for the sake of the children, they decided not to divorce.

By this time Julia sadly realized the day would never come when she would have the type of marriage and home life she had hoped for. One morning, as she considered that the only thing familiar in her life was her feeling of walking alone, this desperate woman determined to *grow* through her alone times rather than grieve through them. She started spending her lonely times reading, writing down her thoughts, and pouring her heart out to God. She soon discovered that her identity was not wrapped up in her circumstances—that is, who she was married to and what was expected of her—but rather, in who she was before a God who loved her. That realization propelled her out of her pit of loneliness and made her want to live again. She began immersing herself in God's Word instead of the television. She began practicing the spiritual disciplines, such as meditating on God's Word and fasting and praying. And for the first time in her life, she found strength and confidence.

Today, Julia is one of the strongest, wisest, and most influential women I know. Professionally, she is the director of adult ministries at a large growing church, a writer and teacher of life-changing Bible studies, and a sought-after speaker who teaches about effectiveness in ministry and intimacy with God. Personally, her warm smile, compassionate eyes, and commanding presence cause women to flock around her with the hopes of learning the secrets to her strength. She and her husband of 50 years have rekindled the flame and have been happily married the past few decades. Although she displays an inner strength uncommon among women, Julia is the first to admit her spiritual muscles didn't develop easily. She walked a long road of aloneness that shaped her into the woman she is today...a woman more stable and capable of handling whatever comes her way. She is a woman who now embraces the alone times because they present to her an opportunity to grow. Julia truly knows what it means to grow stronger as a result of walking alone.

Walking Alone Today

Walking with Busyness

Patricia is a woman who still walks alone. But you'd never know it. With a career in high-rise office real estate, Patricia has money at her disposal, a wealth of experience in world travel, is able to speak several different languages, is married to a professional athlete, and enjoys diverse hobbies such as skydiving and rock climbing. To just about everyone, Patricia has it all. But even with love, money, job fulfillment, independence, and respect, Patricia feels achingly alone.

Because she is the primary "breadwinner" in her home and because she has no children, Patricia often finds she doesn't "fit" into the circles of women in her church, neighborhood, and community. She has little in common with most women and finds she often can't relate or bond with anyone.

"I see the stay-at-home wives in the neighborhood and at church filling this role for their families and I become somewhat bitter," she says. While she'd like to quit her job and have children as well, her husband has never held down a job long enough to support the two of them.

"I feel so terribly alone in my stress as I juggle a leadership position at work, long hours commuting, and tight deadlines, and then come home and have another arena in which I need to excel, like cooking, cleaning, shopping, and keeping a home together.

"It's not that my husband doesn't want to help," she says. "He simply does not possess the skills. So I run myself ragged by leaving the office early to shop and clean, then staying up late working on my computer at home, then racing back to work the next morning. Many times I find myself lonely, sad, and tired."

Because Patricia feels no one understands the stress and pace of her life, she feels alone as a woman. But she is not alone.

Walking with Stress

Kathy walks alone, too. But it's a different kind of aloneness.

Having her adult children move back in with her, and having aging parents who need her time and care, Kathy feels alone in her responsibilities and feels that she has no life of her own. With everyone needing something from her, Kathy feels she is in a desert of aloneness, even though she can barely find a quiet corner in her house. (Just recently, after her father was put in a home for the aging and her adult children moved to a place of their own, Kathy said the changes in her home didn't bring to her life what she had hoped. "The ironic thing is that now that the stress is off and there's just three people in my house instead of nine, I still feel just as alone as I did before.")

Walking Single

Erin walks alone, as well. Coming from a past in which she had several serious dating relationships, she finds it difficult to be in her forties and still single. She fills her days by working, serving in her church, and keeping herself active during the weekends. But she is continually reminded of her aloneness when she is excluded from gatherings and events because she doesn't have a husband, when holidays come and go without someone special to share them with, and when she has to do handyman-type tasks around her home without the help of some extra muscle and hands.

Walking in the Dark

Jini, too, has walked alone as a woman…during a long struggle with infertility. "While my husband was sympathetic, he was too busy and distracted by his job. And *I* was the one who couldn't get pregnant month after month. It was the only time in my life when I felt like 'everyone can do this but me.'" While she knew God was with her, Jini says, "It was still a very lonely time."

And Carla began walking alone in her early twenties when she finally revealed to her family that her sister's husband had molested her. When everyone in her family chose not to believe her and not to deal with the situation, Carla felt betrayed and alone. Feeling that no one (not her parents, not her husband, nor her closest friends) could understand the extent of her pain and anger, she wandered into a desert of emotional aloneness and stayed there for years.

A friend's comment to me one day describes well the aloneness that I think women can feel today even though they are busy and in the midst of people, plans, and noise: "I can be surrounded by people in my life and still feel very much alone."

As women, we walk alone because of the circumstances in our lives, because of the absence of relationships, because of the ways we often don't feel connected with others. We walk alone when we're single or stressed or struggling with something we feel no one else understands. In fact, we walk alone often enough that the Stranger of Aloneness is Someone we should know very well by now.

Walking with the Stranger of Aloneness

Beth is familiar with the Stranger of Aloneness. She's been with Him many times in the deserts of her life. She first met Him during a loveless marriage in which her husband cheated on her a number of times. Then, when she remarried a man who loved her the way God wanted her to be loved, she noticed that the Stranger of Aloneness remained at her side even when her husband had to travel away from home on account of his job.

Just recently, Beth lost both of her parents, her father-in-law, and her only child in a matter of four years. And as I sat across the table from her and listened to her talk of her 26-year-old daughter's last days before succumbing to a brain tumor, Beth's eyes shone with a light and hope that hardly seemed possible, considering the deserts she'd visited.

But in two sentences, she gave me the secret to her strength:

"I've learned to be alone," she said with a soft smile, as if the word *alone* carried with it a precious meaning. "I've learned not to look for a way *out* of the desert, but to learn what God wants to teach me while I'm there."

What's the Secret?

What *does* God want to teach us in the deserts we walk through as women? That we can be like Beth and look loneliness straight in the face—through the death of a marriage or the loss of a child or the disappointments in life that leave us feeling barren—and still have hope in our eyes and joy in our hearts? Perhaps it's not *what* He wants us to see, but *who* He wants us to see.

As Beth testifies, the secret to our strength lies not in our circumstances, but in who we meet in spite of them, and what we learn about Him in the process. The strongest, most capable women I know today are women who have walked alone…women who have visited the deserts in life, met God there, embraced His presence, and waited for what He wanted to reveal to them in that alone time.

Where Do *You* Walk?

What about you? Are you struggling with being alone? What exactly are you struggling with? Are you wanting to be married or wanting to be happy in your marriage? Are you struggling with wanting a child or a career or a certain dream that appears out of reach? Are you struggling with not feeling emotionally connected to someone, or feeling no one understands certain things in your past that have affected your present? Or are you just plain tired of bearing things on your own and you'd like to share the burdens with someone?

I wonder, my friend, what would happen if you embraced that Stranger of Aloneness, seeing Him not as the Stranger who has come to take something from you, but as the Blesser who has come to bestow on you something wonderful!

Usually, when we are in our desert of aloneness, it's difficult to believe something good can actually come of it. After all, we see only broad plains of problems and endless sands of uncertainty. Yet God often meets us at our weakest, most vulnerable times to present to us His plans and bestow on us His blessings. Think about it: the times that we are alone—contemplating our life and away from the distractions of other people—could be the times that we are most in the mind-set to listen to what He wants to say to us. Yet I wonder how often God comes to meet us in our lonely darkness to reveal His plans for us only to find us preoccupied with getting out of the dark, lonely night and into the day that we struggle with Him—or our circumstances—and miss the blessing He has for us. Perhaps when God sends a messenger to give us hope, we beat down that hope and choose to dwell on the negative. Maybe when God gets us alone to speak to our hearts, we find a way to bring noise or people or *something* into the situation so we don't feel so alone. Or maybe when God nudges at our hearts to go away with Him alone, we find a reason to resist…looking to someone or something to turn to instead. We struggle with Him and we miss out on the blessings He wants to give us.

Counting the Blessings

We know from God's Word that ultimately all things work together for good to those who love Him (Romans 8:28). And in His Word, there are many things He promised to us, long ago, that He still intends to deliver. In Jeremiah 29:11, God says, "I know the plans I have for you…plans to prosper you and not to harm you, plans to give you hope and a future." While God made this promise to the nation of Israel, we can be certain that because we are His children, He cares about our future, too. And why does God have these plans for us? Is there a certain response He's hoping to receive from you and me? You bet! Verses 12-14 tell us why He intends good for us: "Then you will call upon me and come and pray to me, and I will listen to you. You will seek me and find me when you seek me with all your heart. I will be found by you…and will bring you back from captivity" (or your desert of loneliness).

God has plans for us and He desires that we call upon Him, get to know Him, trust Him, and live intimately with Him so we can carry out those plans. Perhaps He has allowed our venture into the desert so that He can talk with us uninterrupted and lead us to a place of fulfillment and strength in Him. I don't know about you, but when

I'm in the desert of aloneness, it's because not too many other people are talking to me, and that's the time I can hear God's voice the clearest. On the other hand, when I'm in a place of abundance and things are going well in my life, I tend to not listen and long for God's voice as much.

God not only has plans for us, but He wants us to be able to live them out...a strong indication that you and I will not die in our desert of aloneness. We are told in Ephesians 2:10 that we are "God's workmanship, created in Christ Jesus to do good works, which God prepared *in advance* for us to do" (emphasis added). If we were created for good works that God already planned for us to accomplish, then surely God isn't out to destroy our lives so we can't perform them. No! He wants us to be fulfilled and walking according to His plan. But *His plan* is the key here—not ours.

His Plans, Not My Own

I had to learn this concept in my own life many years ago when I was struggling in the desert of wanting—and waiting for—a second child. When our daughter, Dana, was a year old, my husband and I decided we were ready to start trying for another child. Since I was able to get pregnant with our little Dana right away, we figured we could have our second child right "on schedule" like the first. But when month after month went by and I did not become pregnant, we became concerned that something might be wrong and consulted a doctor. My doctor, and several well-meaning friends, told us to relax and the baby would come in time. But after a couple more years, there was still no baby.

One summer morning, as I was sitting out on the back patio of our home, I began to pray through God's promises to me in Scripture, asking God to keep those promises by giving me a long-awaited second child.

I reminded God of His promise in Jeremiah 29:11 to give me a future and a hope. I reminded Him of Psalm 37:4, in which He tells me to delight in Him and He will give me the desires of my heart.

And I reminded Him of Psalm 84:11, in which He promises "no good thing does He withhold from those who walk uprightly" (NASB).

Then I had to stop! God's promises to prosper me, give me the desires of my heart, and not withhold anything good for me didn't necessarily mean He was promising me another baby. Yes, God promised to prosper me (and I assumed that prospering meant giving me another child). But what was *His* idea of prospering me? He promised to give me a future (and I assumed that future would be with another child), but what was *His* plan for my future? He promised to not withhold anything good, but what exactly was *His* perspective of good? Upon realizing that I was assuming my desires were the same as God's, I spent the next few soul-searching days in prayer, asking God what *He* wanted of my life, what *His* future plans for me might hold, what *He* considered "good" for my life.

During those next few days, God reminded me of my longtime desire to write books. From the time I was a child, I had a mind-set to be a writer. Then as I became an adult, the desire was to write books that encouraged women. I had hoped to write a few books after Dana was born, but life as a young mother got so hectic, the books never got written. Now here I was, still hoping to write, and asking God for another baby! I told the Lord that deep in my heart my desire was still to write, even if it meant not having another baby. That day I surrendered to the Lord my desire to have a second child. And to this day, the second child has never come. But the second book is what you're reading. And there have been nine more books since. God did have a future for me—just not the one I was trying to engineer!

Within a couple days of surrendering my desire for a second child, the doctor called me with the results of some fertility tests my husband and I had taken. "You know that miracle baby you've been praying for?" the doctor said to me. "Well you already had her, three years ago!" The doctor explained there was fertility incompatibility between my husband and myself and we shouldn't have been able to have *any* children at all!

To this day, I find it touching that the Blesser came to meet me in my desert of aloneness as I was waiting for a second child. And the message He came to deliver to me was that I already had been given my blessing (when Dana was born a few years earlier) and I was about to discover a new arena of blessing (through writing and speaking) that He had stored up for me. I'm thankful for *His* plans, not my own. And I'm thankful that He led me to that place alone, where His news would be received as a blessing, rather than something bitter.

What's *Your* Blessed News?

So, what might the Blesser be coming to tell *you* in your desert of aloneness? That now that your husband is gone, He wants to be your husband? That your infertility is for a reason? That you've lost that position or person or place because He has a new direction for you? That He wants to meet you in a new way during this season of aloneness? It may be something that you had no intention of ever even asking for...but if it's coming from the hand of God, then it is truly good.

My friend, the Blesser has something to show you, something to say. He has allowed you into this desert of yours for a reason, and from His perspective, it's a good one. This God in heaven has plans for you—plans to prosper you and give you a hope and future. Do you believe that? Do you want to get a glimpse of what those plans are and what that future might hold? Then stop struggling...and let Him speak.

You may be amazed at what He has to say.

Embracing the Blessing

For Personal Application

1. Surrendering the struggle against loneliness first involves surrendering to God—in every way. If you haven't yet given your heart and life to Him, read "Surrendering the Struggle" on page 211.

2. Make a list of the "good" things in your life right now. How has God blessed you already? Now consider that you might not enjoy these good things if God had given you an entirely different life than you have now. With that in mind, thank Him for your current situation of walking alone.

3. Take to God that area of aloneness that you struggle with and surrender it to Him, asking Him to show you the blessings that lie therein. Then, invite Him to stay with you in the desert and help you to find Him in this season of searching.

4. Share with another woman this week your experience in the alone times and where God met you.

For Further Study

Read the following verses and list some of the ways that God intends to bless you, based on these verses:

Jeremiah 29:11-13:

Psalm 37:4:

Romans 8:28-29:

Psalm 84:11:

Alone at Heart:
LOOKING TO YOUR HEAVENLY HUSBAND

Married or not, I think we all, at one time or another, feel alone at heart.

Sandy is single, and she's felt that way many times.

"I don't *like* being single," she told me one day with tears in her eyes. "I've always wanted to be a wife and a mother and I can't imagine that God wouldn't have that in store for me."

Sandy has heard all the classic lines:

Trust in God's timing, not your own.
Focus on your relationship with God and then He'll give you
*   a relationship with a man.*
When you stop looking for love, you'll find it.

But the lines aren't helping anymore. And now that Sandy is well into her thirties, she's frightened that her possibilities of finding someone at this point in life are growing gravely slimmer.

"The worst thing, I think, is coming home at night to an empty house and walking through the door into the silence," she told me. "There's no one to welcome me, no one to be excited that I'm there." Sandy knows in her head that God is there, but she still feels alone at heart.

Vickie is alone at heart as well. But she has been married for 40 years. She admits that when she married at 18 years old, she never imagined she would ever feel alone. But living with a man who tends to distance himself from her emotionally whenever there is conflict, stress, or he feels overwhelmed, has left Vickie walking alone through much of her marriage. "Sometimes my husband can detach himself from me emotionally to where it's like a divorce," she says. Vickie and her husband are continually in counseling, working through the years of "stacked up stuff that hasn't been resolved." And they are both determined to see their marriage through. But in the meantime, Vickie looks to God to fill that hunger in her heart for a connection and a feeling that she is not alone.

Theresa is alone at heart, too. She left her marriage a few years ago when her husband wouldn't get help for his alcohol and abuse problems. Although she admits she's better off without him, her pain of aloneness intensifies when she thinks of her ex-husband, who is now living with someone else. "Why does *he* have someone, while *I'm* still alone?" she asked me one day. "It just isn't fair."

Whether we long for a husband, or long to be emotionally connected to the one we already have, we need to know that we *can* know fulfillment in the midst of our aloneness.

Sorting Out the Myths

From the time most of us were little girls, we heard that our key to happiness was to fall in love, marry, and live happily ever after. And so, from the time we're fed the fairy tale, we convince ourselves that as long as we find someone to share our life with, we will never walk alone. But it just isn't true. Ask Vickie. And Theresa. And me.

If we marry a man who travels often or is consumed with his job, we may find ourselves feeling alone. If we marry a man who seldom communicates or won't make an emotional connection with us, we may feel alone. If we never marry, or we find ourselves eventually divorced or widowed, we may feel alone.

I believe it's because we, as women, were made for relationships. And so if our life is lacking in them, we tend to feel incomplete.

No One to Help

When God created the first woman, He intended for her to be a helper. In fact, God said, "It is not good for the man to be alone. I will make a helper suitable for him" (Genesis 2:18). So, God made women to be helpers, partners, companions, encouragers, lovers, friends. Because our very nature is to be a helper, it can become a source of frustration for us, at times, if no one enters our life who *needs* our help, when someone we love no longer *wants* our help, when our children think they are better off *without* our help, when we find we are *no longer* a help, or when we become overwhelmed with people we feel we *can't* help. So, what's a helpless woman to do?

We also know that God created us, as women, in His image (Genesis 1:27), and so our nature to love and be loved completely not only reflects God's characteristics, but His perfect design for us as well. But God knew good and well that men in and of themselves would not be able to completely fill our emotional tank. In fact, I think He was planning on it. I think by making us with needs that only He could fill, He was reserving a place in our hearts for Him alone.[1] Perhaps He was placing in us a well so deep that only He could fill it, and that way, married or not, we would be neither content nor complete until we were in close relationship with Him.

We know from Scripture that God is a jealous God (Exodus 20:4-5) and He will be second to no man in our lives. He demands—and deserves—to be first place in our hearts. To you and me, He wants to be *the Man*...the One who keeps us from feeling alone at heart.

Let me share with you the story of a woman who was unloved and unfulfilled in her marriage and came to see how God could be *the Man* in her life. Whether you're looking for love or lonely in love, I think you'll be able to relate. Her name was Leah, and we find her story in the Bible.

Leah's Story

Leah most likely had hopes and dreams of being happily married, just like every other woman of her day (and ours). All she wanted was for her husband, Jacob, to love her. But Jacob loved Leah's sister, Rachel. And not only did Leah live with that hurt, but she was probably reminded daily of how she was second best to her beautiful younger sister.

Poor Leah! Her husband was tricked into marrying her in the first place, a ploy concocted by her father, who perhaps figured no man would choose his older daughter, Leah, on his own. So on Jacob and Rachel's wedding night, Leah's father made the girls switch places, and when Jacob awoke the next morning to find Leah in his bed, he was furious. I imagine it ripped a hole into Leah's heart to hear her new husband complain that he'd gotten her instead, after giving her all to him the night before. Perhaps day after day she heard of all the reasons her husband would rather be with Rachel than with her. Leah probably carried some deep hurts in her heart, as I imagine any woman would who has to hear of her shortcomings and why her husband would prefer to be with someone else! But through all this, Leah didn't give up. She was determined to do whatever it took to win her husband's heart. And she believed that meant giving him a son.

We're told in the Bible that God saw that Leah was unloved, so He allowed her to conceive a child (Genesis 29:31). When Leah bore her first son, she said, "It is because the LORD has seen my misery. Surely my husband will love me now." But Jacob's love didn't follow. So Leah had another son. And another. And after bearing that third son, she again hoped that would do the trick, saying, "Surely my husband will love me now." But still, he didn't.

After giving Jacob a fourth son, and seeing that her husband still favored Rachel, Leah simply said, "This time I will praise the LORD" (Genesis 29:35).

I love how Leah's focus finally shifted. No longer did she seek after her husband's love; instead, she looked to the Lord who loved her. (And, incidentally, it was that fourth son, named Judah, that God chose as the bloodline through whom His Son, Jesus, would eventually be born. Could it be that God's reward followed when Leah finally gained her focus?)

A few years later, Leah bore two more sons and a daughter, and her last comment was not that her husband would love her, but that Jacob would "treat me with honor." Maybe by then Leah knew that her husband's love and devotion was simply out of reach. And perhaps she learned, after many attempts and no success, to quit striving after the heart of the one she would never win and to start living for the One who had always loved her.

We can safely assume that it was Leah's desert experience of lovelessness from her husband that drove her to find an oasis of love from God and begin to look to Him as the heavenly Husband she could live for. Perhaps the love she found in God convinced her that He was real. I say that because later, when Jacob and his wives and all their children moved, it was Rachel—not Leah—who took along the family idols (Genesis 31:17-19,34). Perhaps Leah had experienced God in such a real and personal way that she didn't seek her fulfillment anywhere else. And unlike Rachel, Leah became devoted to her God rather than the wooden objects her father had taught her to worship.

And because Leah's son, Judah, was chosen to continue the bloodline from which Jesus came, we can assume the Almighty looked favorably on the one who loved her husband even though she received no love in return, the one who was a faithful wife in spite of how she was treated. Apparently God made up for what Leah lacked in her marriage by giving her eternal blessings instead.

Finding a New Focus

Now I realize that my reference to eternal blessings may not make you feel any better if you are struggling with feeling disconnected to your husband, or struggling with not having a husband at all. But let me encourage you with this: A marriage here on earth is temporary. It will last, at the most, until you or your spouse dies. But marriage with the Lord will last into eternity. And I've found that in my own experiences of being lonely in love (for the most part, married to a pastor who is an introvert and very busy in ministry), focusing on my heavenly Husband is one sure way to get my mind off of unmet expectations in my earthly marriage and to still live in joy as a woman much loved.

So what is all this talk about a marriage to the Lord?

Throughout the Old Testament, God refers to His chosen people, the nation of Israel, as His bride. In Isaiah 54:5, He tells Israel, "Your Maker is your husband—the LORD Almighty is His name." In the New Testament, Jesus refers to Himself as the Bridegroom and to His church (those who trust Him as Savior and Lord) as His bride. Jesus also talked of going away to prepare a home for us in heaven and then returning to get us, His bride, to take us back to live with Him (see John 14:2-3). God's comparison of His love for us with a husband-wife relationship is too obvious to overlook in Scripture; He is definitely trying to make a point to us.

Putting Marriage in Its Proper Place

Could that point be that God wants us to see Him as our heavenly Husband and the One who holds our hope and future in His hands? I believe so. Of course, upon making a marriage vow to God and to our spouse, there's no question that we should make our marriage relationship a priority over any other relationship here on earth (even that of our children) and do all that is humanly possible to make it work until death do us part. But if our perspective were realigned so that we, as women, considered ourselves married to God *first*, it would dramatically change how we view our earthly marriage or lack of one.

This was apparently the case with Geri. Geri was a strikingly beautiful woman who approached me one morning after a speaking event. I had just encouraged a large group of women to listen to the call that Jesus, their heavenly Husband, was making on their life—the call to come back to His heart and live a life of intimacy with Him.

As Geri approached me, I could see that she had tears in her eyes. "My husband left me three years ago," she said. "Today would have been our twentieth wedding anniversary."

I reached out to touch her hand as she continued: "I was praying last night that my husband would call me today. That's all I wanted—just a call." Geri stopped to regain her composure and then said: "I realize now that God answered my prayer. My Husband *was* calling me today." Her smile and the tears of joy in her eyes told me she now understood, for the first time in three painful years, who her real Husband was. She left with a new hope that morning...a hope founded in knowing that she was loved and cherished by the One who would never leave her.

Jesus told us that marriage on this earth is for a lifetime, not for eternity (Matthew 22:30). Upon the death of you or your spouse, it will end. (And unfortunately in many cases, a marriage ends a lot earlier than that, through abandonment or divorce.) Your marriage to Christ, however, is eternal. In fact, your relationship with Him here on earth is similar to an engagement period, and the real marriage will take place in heaven. Jesus told us that when we meet Him in heaven, we will partake in the "marriage supper" (Revelation 19:9). Whose marriage? *Our* marriage with the Lord.

Picturing a Perfect Marriage

What will our marriage with the Lord be like? I believe God designed marriage between a man and woman here on earth to give us a glimpse of what a marriage with Christ can be like in heaven. Try to go with me here: A marriage with Christ will be a perfect union of unconditional love and trust, complete vulnerability, sensitivity, tenderness, security, provision, and fulfillment. It will also be completely free of any of the negatives that we may have experienced in our own earthly marriage or other people's marriages. That's because our marriage in heaven will be to the Perfect One, Jesus Christ, who knows only goodness, faithfulness, and love. In a marriage to Christ, you are treated as the most precious, beautiful, sought-after bride there ever was. Because in His eyes, you are.

Now, if you think of a husband in terms of a sexual relationship, you won't have a right picture of marriage to God, for it won't be a sexual relationship. Instead, think of God as a husband in terms of the biblical role and responsibilities a husband has. For instance, a husband is to provide, protect, comfort, encourage, befriend, and love…and God does all of that! And because He is perfect and without sin, He can do all of that a lot better than any human husband could!

When I speak of the Lord being our Husband, I'm not suggesting we ignore or think less of our earthly husbands. And I am by no means suggesting we give up on them or get out of our marriages. To the contrary, I am suggesting that we take certain expectations off of our husbands and leave them with the Lord, as a way of showing our husbands how much we *do* love them. And when we lessen the load of expectations on our husbands, it often frees up our husbands to love us in the best way they can…without unrealistic expectations being held over their heads.

Great Expectations

My sister recently attended a marriage conference in which the couples were told by the speakers that there is only one person who can meet all of their emotional needs, and that was their spouse. Furthermore, the husbands were told that it was their duty to heal the hurts of their wife's past and make her into the whole, confident, and fulfilled woman she was intended by God to be.

Wow! What a task. I imagine those men left that conference with a pretty heavy burden of responsibility on their shoulders—one that they probably will soon discover they cannot carry. I imagine, too, that those wives are in for some pretty stark disappointments as they realize the truth of Jeremiah 17:5-6, which tells us that when we depend on people—or our husbands—for our fulfillment, we will live like stony wastes in the wilderness. In other words, we'll be like dried-out bushes or tumbleweeds that blow here and there to whomever will love us. The fact is—and both Scripture and experience make this clear—that no man or woman can completely fill another person's emotional tank. That's a God-sized task meant for…well, God!

Secret to Success

I have found in my own marriage that when my husband tries to meet my long list of emotional expectations, he gets frustrated with how far he falls short. But not as frustrated as me! And I've also found that when I take those expectations off of Hugh and leave them with the Lord where they belong, it frees up Hugh to love me in the way that he can, without guilt or feelings of "not measuring up" in my book. Furthermore, as I concentrate more fully on my marriage to God, and I pursue my husband less, it makes Hugh want to pursue me a little more. (I think that's a guy-thing!) And it makes our marriage to each other less of a weighty obligation and more of a willful inspiration. As I fall more in love with Jesus, He gives me more of a love for my husband, as well...but a love free of demands and disappointments.

Focusing on Your First Love

My friend, where are *you* concentrating your energy when it comes to your love life? Is Jesus your first love? He's going to be your Husband into eternity. Don't you want to spend life here on earth in a wonderful engagement to Him so that when you get to heaven you two can pick up where you left off?

I remember the four months I was engaged to Hugh. We had a long-distance dating relationship, so the few times we saw each other really meant a lot to us. We dreamed of the moment we would say, "I do" to each other and never again have to be away from each other, not even for a day! (We actually made that promise to each other as so many lovebirds do!) I remember feeling, between visits, that I would just die if I couldn't be with Hugh soon. I longed for the day I would be his wife and we would no longer have to be separated by physical distance.

Obviously, we weren't able to keep that promise of never being separated again. My travels as a speaker and my husband's position in ministry have many times not afforded us the opportunity— or luxury— of taking our business trips together.

And in fact, as I wrote the first edition of this book, he was in Papua New Guinea, on a two-week stay in the jungle, away from any telephones, modems, or postal services to "keep in touch." Since then, he has explored a few other countries for two weeks at a time and put me through some long uncomfortable hours as he was "not heard from" while scaling some of the highest mountain peaks in those countries. Keeping a vow of never being separated physically wasn't realistic because of our ministry obligations and his backpacking hobby, yet our love for each other still makes separation difficult.

Do you and I feel a similar longing when it comes to our heavenly Husband? Do you and I long for the day we will be joined to our Lover and Lord forever? We *should* have that kind of longing in our hearts. And when we make our relationship with Christ a priority and make Him our focal point in all things, we will know true fulfillment— even in the alone times.

Let me share with you three practical things that we can do— every day—in our relationship with the Lord so that our marriage to Him fills the void a man cannot fill.

1. *Communicate with God about everything.* Relationships are built and maintained upon communication. And a lot of times that starts with talking about the little things and building up to a more vulnerable and soul-exposing communication. Tell God about the little things in your day, every day. Unlike some husbands, He will be glad to hear every little detail. (God never tells us, "Get to the point, please!") As you go to God first with everything on your heart and mind, you may find you have less to complain or talk about with your husband, which may make you a little more attractive to him and more of a mystery to him, as well. (And don't most men love a good mystery?)

   I find that when I talk to God more, and to Hugh less, it causes Hugh to be more interested in my life and more interested in wanting to talk with me. It is a breath of fresh air in my marriage for *my husband* to be the one to say, "Let's spend some time together so we can catch up on life." And if you're not married, telling God about your day is one way of letting Him fill that need for "someone to talk to" and "someone to listen."

2. *Commit yourself to trusting in God alone.* Trust is another key element in a good relationship. And God wants you to trust Him as the One who will provide for you, protect you, and advise you in various matters, just as you would look to a husband to do the same. Look to God's Word for direction in that big decision you need to make. Wait upon Him for guidance in those smaller decisions, too. Trust God's promises, in His Word, to provide for you financially and otherwise when things get tight. Unlike an earthly husband, God has unlimited assets. (Psalm 50:10 tells us He owns the cattle on a thousand hills!) He has all the resources you will ever need when you get into a bind.

God is also all-knowing, so nothing takes Him by surprise. Furthermore, He isn't capable of making a mistake, so He'll never drop the ball. Plus, He's got perfect timing, so you don't have to worry about missing anything. Doesn't that already relieve a little bit of the relational pressure that might exist in your marriage? Instead of depending on your husband for everything, start putting things in God's hands. And if you're not married, doesn't that make you feel a little more secure already, knowing you're not alone—that you have Someone who can pick up the loose ends in your life and help you out?

3. *Consider your life with God a partnership.* If you're married, chances are you share just about everything from money to living quarters to possessions. The same works with being "married" to God, only it's more like everything belongs to

Him, but He gives you access. Share with Him your time, your plans, your finances, your love, your thoughts, your concerns, your devotion, and your loyalty, and you will never have to worry that anything you give Him will be misused, abused, misplaced, or taken for granted.

My friend Lee, now a 70-year-old divorcee, lives out this concept of a marriage, a daily partnership, with God. But it didn't happen overnight. For several years, Lee believed she had to have a husband in order to be happy and complete. So she went in and out of marriages looking for fulfillment. Two divorces and a death later, Lee found herself more alone at heart than she had ever been. But the day her eyes were opened to her First Love was the day her life changed forever.

Lee came face-to-face with the fact that her heavenly Husband, Jesus Christ, gave His life for her so she could live with Him forever. She realized no man she had ever known or would know would do such a thing for her. Lee began to spend more time in God's Word, reading about His character and love. She soon joined a Bible study at her church and began meeting with other women who were lonely at heart but in love with the Lord Jesus. Gradually, her focus shifted from looking for another heartbreaker to loving the Heart Healer. Today, Lee walks tall as an attractive, confident woman who is very much in love...with her Lord. She wears a gold ring—that her children gave her—on the fourth finger of her left hand, to remind her of her commitment and "marriage" to the One who loves her most. Lee is a beautiful example of a wounded woman who was made happy and whole in a love relationship with her heavenly Husband.

Although there are times when Lee still feels lonely in that quiet house of hers, God ministers to her in ways that a person couldn't, giving her a peace that comforts her soul and a joy that fills her heart.

"Since I recommitted my heart to Jesus," Lee says, "I still feel a bit lonely at times, but I never feel *alone* anymore—not like I did when I was searching for love apart from God. The Lord has made such a difference in the way I look at life and love and being alone."

His Promise to Us

God's Word contains a special promise to women like Lee who take Him up on His offer to be their heavenly Husband. His promise is that no matter how lonely you may feel, He will fill up your heart and your home with His presence.

In Psalm 68:5, God is described as "a father of the fatherless, a defender of the widow." And verse 6 adds, "God makes a home for the lonely" (NASB).

Did you catch that? It is *His* comforting presence that warms up your house and makes it a home. It is *His* sweet presence that greets you as you walk through the door at the end of the day. It is *His* calming presence that sings over you, allowing you to sleep at night.[2] Now that's the kind of home that *any* woman would want…a home in which she no longer feels alone.

If you, my friend, have found yourself in the desert of aloneness—no matter what the reason—remember that you are not alone. God is with you, and He can fill that hollow in your heart.

So tell me, do you want His presence to warm your house? Do you want Him to be your companion—not only in the alone moments, but always? Do you want to live as a wife much-loved?

God promises to care for you. Won't you let Him be *your* heavenly Husband?

Standing Tall as a Bride of Christ

For Personal Application

1. If you're single, write out a description of the perfect husband. (Go ahead, dream a little.)

Now, take that list of characteristics and see how the Lord fits the bill for what you need in a husband. Thank Him for being there for you and ask Him to help you live in this "marriage."

2. Whether you're single or married, consider writing some marriage vows to the Lord. Do you promise to love Him for better or for worse, richer or poorer, in sickness and in health? You may find it helpful to think of commitment to God as being similar to a marriage commitment. Prayerfully ask Him what He would like you to pledge and then do it.

My vows to the Lord:

3. Find another woman who is lonely in love (you probably won't have to look far) and encourage her with what you've read in this chapter or discovered in God's Word about His desire to be our heavenly Husband. As you invest your life in others, the encouragement will come back around toward you.

4. Every morning when you get up, look in the mirror and determine to do what you can to look and be your best for your heavenly Husband. When God becomes the One you seek to please, others may discover how you are becoming more pleasing.

For Further Study

Read Jeremiah 17:5-6. What does this passage say about depending on a man (or anyone else) for all that you need emotionally?

Now look at Jeremiah 17:7-8. What are the blessings that God pours into your life as you look to Him for strength?

Read Genesis 29:14-35. What is the one area of your life in which you need to finally say—as Leah did—"This time I will praise the Lord"?

Read the following verses and note next to each one how God "husbands" you in a way that an earthly husband is not capable of:

Romans 8:39:

Psalm 62:8:

Psalm 139:1-2:

Psalm 139:3:

Psalm 139:7-10:

Psalm 147:3:

If you're married, notice the ways the Lord can meet your needs that your husband hasn't been able to. Then, rather than grow resentful toward your husband, thank God for His unconditional love and ask Him to help you release the expectations that you've had of your earthly husband and leave them with your heavenly Husband, where they belong. Then thank God for the things that your earthly husband is capable of. (You may find new reasons to love him!)

If you're single, focus on the ways God can love you that an earthly husband never could, and ask God to cement in your heart a commitment to depending on Him, rather than looking to a man or someone else to fill the places only God can satisfy.

Take a moment now to pray, and praise God for being the perfect Husband and ask Him to help you keep your eyes focused on Him, and not anyone else.

3

Alone as a Parent:
PARTNERING WITH GOD

*D*esiree never thought she would be a single parent. But then, who does?

When she married Jim ten years earlier, everything looked like it would be fine. But shortly after the children came, Jim's irrational behavior became evidence of his drug and alcohol addictions. Desiree soon found herself living like a single parent while her husband was in and out of drug recovery programs and eventually in and out of jail for spousal abuse. After much prayer on Desiree's part—and many threats, apologies, and empty promises on Jim's part—Desiree secured a restraining order against Jim and started the long lonely road of permanently parenting alone.

Desiree admits that some days she feels very lonely. And she has days that she gets frustrated about being the only adult in charge of her children's diverse schedules, activities, homework projects, and all the other responsibilities that parenting includes. But Desiree found it helpful when she came to realize that as a parent, she is never really alone. For the first time in her life, she recognized she was partnering with God in the parenting of her children. And she is letting God be the "Dad" that her children never really had.

Whether you are raising a child by yourself, or just feel like you are because of a lack of support or involvement from a spouse, parenting can be a long, lonely road. Sometimes we feel alone in carrying the spiritual torch for our children; sometimes we find out something about our children that we feel we can't share. I know many mothers who feel they walk alone because their adult children are living in rebellion and messing up so many lives. Virtually all of us know a woman with an unwed daughter—or son—who is expecting a baby, or a woman with a child on drugs, a child behind bars, a child running from the law, or a child running from the Lord. And these are the more serious situations. Even in a family where children are generally obedient and there are close family ties we can have moments when we feel all alone as a parent.

Julia (whose story is in chapter 1) remembers parenting alone for several years when her husband was on the road speaking and traveling. At times he was gone as many as 25 days out of a month, so she and the children rarely saw him. "I felt very alone dealing with the teenagers myself," she said. Her two oldest were especially rebellious and she felt overwhelmed with the responsibility and the helpless feeling of not knowing what to do. She found it hard to enforce the rules by herself and to keep up with the different worlds of four very different children. "Their father would lay down the law and yell a lot when he was home, but then he'd leave and I was left to enforce his rules." Julia often felt like a single mother as she sat in church and at school programs by herself, did all the shopping and home chores, took care of the car and yard, and learned to do home repairs by herself. In many ways, she learned to be the "Dad" of the house, making quick decisions and taking charge.

Hidden Blessings

The role of parenting was never meant for one person alone. But today, an increasing number of women bear the weight of that burden. Today, more than 9 percent of American households are run by single parents. And the US Census Bureau reports that there are ten million single *mothers* living with children under 18 today, as opposed to just three million in 1970. I believe God's heart extends toward women who—whether through singleness or through an absent husband—are raising the children on their own. One way I believe He exhibits this is by causing blessings to come out of the bitterness of single parenting. For instance, there are some special things that can happen in spite of parenting alone.

Some of the people I know who have the closest relationships with their mothers were once children being raised alone by their moms. Either their parents were divorced when they were children, their father died early in life, they never knew their dad, or his presence just wasn't felt in their home. For some reason or another, it was just the kids and mom, and that bond was special.

My friend, Christi, lost her father when she was 11, but kept a closeness with her mother that continues to this day. In many ways Christi and her mom were all each other had, for Christi's older brothers and sister had married and left home by the time their mom was widowed. And now that Christi, who is single, has adopted a couple of children of her own, she is encouraged that perhaps they will share a similar closeness, too. Although the burden of single parenting is great at times—because she has no help in the middle of the night when her daughters are sick, or she can't keep up with the demands of her job, caring for her home, and watching her daughters—she admits that she has opportunities her friends don't have because she is the only parent in her children's life. "Not having to spread yourself between a husband *and* children is one way of looking on the bright side," she says. Christi also admits that because she doesn't have a husband to depend on, she must depend on the Lord all the more. That has made her stronger in her faith and trust and stronger in her confidence as a mother, because she is learning to partner with God.

Desiree is also noticing some hidden blessings of parenting alone—primarily the fact that she is growing stronger in her relationship with God now that she is looking to Him to help her. And she is learning to enjoy the quiet times with God that she didn't have when her children's father was living (or raging) in the home.

"I think the quiet times alone with God, when the kids are in bed, and the television is off, and every other voice is silenced, is when I've really touched the hem of His garment and been close to the Lord," Desiree says. "I now have a renewed outlook on life, knowing that it's not going to be perfect and my circumstances aren't what I expected them to be. But the Lord is with me, which makes all the difference in the world."

Desiree learned early on that regrets will only turn into bitterness, which is stifling as a woman and a mother. "God has been teaching me to enjoy my life because it's the only one I'm going to get. He's been reminding me not to look at the past (like before I had kids or when I had a husband in the house) as 'the good old days' but to make the present the 'good old days.'"

Desiree's perspective is worth imitating: "Every single day I have a choice of how to live my life. I can't choose what life will bring me, but I *can* choose whether I will live it in victory or defeat. Today I'm choosing victory."

She has to, because little eyes are watching.

"Through all the difficulties I've faced, I have learned the faithfulness and mercy of God. And I experienced the comfort of the Holy Spirit."

By walking alone as a parent, Desiree has "seen God" in her time of need, experienced His presence during the quiet moments, and sought His direction during the difficult times. She's partnered with Him. And she's learned to let Him be the support, direction, comfort, and guidance that she, as well as her children, needs.

As I said before, God's heart goes out to the woman who finds herself alone as a parent. In fact, we find a touching example of this in the Bible, where we meet a woman—a single mother—who was in dire straits and was encouraged when God made known to her His presence, His power, and His peace.

Hagar's Story

God promised Abraham and Sarah that He would give them a child, and that from that child would come a whole nation. But as the years went by and Abraham and Sarah remained childless well past their childbearing years, Sarah became desperate and gave her Egyptian maid, Hagar, to Abraham in the hope that she could help bear that promised child. When Hagar became pregnant Sarah mistreated her, and Hagar fled to the desert. While there, she met God, and He told her that He saw her situation, the abuse she had received, and her plight. He told her to go back home, submit to her master, and bear the child because God had plans for that child.[1]

Hagar, in response to God's affirmation that He saw her plight and cared for her, called the place "El Roi," meaning, "the God who sees." She came to know God as just that: the God who sees her anguish, her abuse, her agony. She came to experience Him as the One who knew all about her and all about the child she was carrying and the One who assured her that all would be okay. After her encounter with "the God who sees," Hagar gained the strength to get up off the ground, go back to her home, and bear the child. Evidently, just knowing that God saw and understood her situation gave her the courage to face life as a single parent.

But 12 years later, when a child was born to Sarah, Hagar and her child Ishmael got relegated to second class and thrown out of the home.

"Get rid of that slave woman and her son," Sarah shouted to Abraham one day when she caught Ishmael bullying her beloved Isaac, "for that slave woman's son will never share in the inheritance with my son Isaac" (Genesis 21:10).

After those stinging words, Hagar hit the road again, along with her child. Taking only a skin of water and some food that Abraham had given them early that morning, they wandered on foot in the desert. But after a while, they had no place to go, no provisions to eat or drink, no protection from the desert sun or the cold desert nights. When they ran out of water, Hagar put Ishmael under a shaded bush and walked away, saying, "I cannot bear to watch him die." She fell to the ground nearby and sobbed. But "the God who sees" never took His eyes off of her...or her child.

An angel of God called to Hagar and said to her, "What's the matter, Hagar? Do not be afraid; God has heard the boy crying as he lies there. Lift the boy up and take him by the hand, for I will make him into a great nation." God then opened Hagar's eyes "and she saw a well of water. So she went and filled the skin with water and gave the boy a drink."

Hagar and Ishmael made it after all. The story ends on this note: "God was with the boy as he grew up. He lived in the desert and became an archer" (Genesis 21:20). And his mother eventually found a wife for him from her homeland of Egypt (verse 21).

God's Provision for the Single Parent

I believe God included this story in His Word as a source of encouragement to mothers throughout time who would feel they walk alone. In this tender exchange between God and Hagar in the desert, I see *a God who knows a mother by name* and cares about what she's going through. I see *a God who hears a mother's cry*—and her child's cry as well—and responds compassionately. I see *a God who provides*—when a single mom believes she is out of hope and help. And I see *a God who tenderly cares* for a fatherless child so that he has a future and a hope. Let's walk through this story again and look at the promises that you can hold on to.

God Knows You by Name

Hagar had been hopeless in the desert once before, and God had called her by name. The second time, God again calls her by name and says, "What's the matter?" I love that. God *knows* what's the matter, yet He asks—just as a loving father would ask his shy, timid daughter and wait for her to pour her heart out and cry on his shoulder. God is asking His heartbroken daughter to tell Him all about it.

God Sees Your Fears

After asking her what was the matter, God tells Hagar to not be afraid. Hagar *shouldn't* be afraid; she's heard from this God before.

And the first encounter gave her the strength and confidence she needed to go back and face a potentially painful situation. But perhaps now Hagar believes it's all over. Maybe she believes there are no second chances and there is no more hope. Perhaps she has forgotten that this loving "God who sees" still sees and still cares. Maybe life had been going smoothly all those years at the house after her first encounter with God, and she had gradually forgotten about God and failed to turn to Him for help. Yet God takes the initiative to come to *her* in the desert and offer His help. He knows that she thinks it's over, that she's afraid they'll die of starvation, that she is regretting ever bringing a child into the world whom she cannot provide for. He knows all that. And gently, He says, "Do not be afraid; God has heard…"

God Lovingly Offers Advice

God tells Hagar to "lift the boy up and take him by the hand" (Genesis 21:18). God knows that Hagar is the only one that little Ishmael has from this point on. And He admonishes and encourages her to rise to the task. It's as if God were saying, "Your child needs you, so be strong. You can do it."

Notice how Hagar doesn't argue with God. She didn't say…

"But he should have a father in his life to pick him up and take him by the hand."

"What can I do? I don't even have a job!"

"What do I know about teaching him how to be a man?"

"How will I provide for him and protect him in this unfriendly world…out here in this desert?"

No, Hagar didn't argue with God. Perhaps it was the last part of God's statement in verse 18 that instilled in her the confidence she needed: "…for I will make him into a great nation."

Hagar had heard a similar promise to Isaac, probably every day of her own son's life. Yet Sarah's harsh words before they were thrown out of the house ("That slave woman's son will never share in the inheritance with my son Isaac.") probably still rang in her ears. Imagine being told that your child or children will never have anything in their lives…never be taken care of, never! No wonder Hagar wished she and her son could die! She'd rather die than see her child suffer or go without.

Yet God told Hagar He would make Ishmael into a great nation, too. God had a plan for Hagar's child as well.

God Opens Your Eyes to See His Provision

Finally, God opened Hagar's eyes and she saw water (Genesis 21:19). The verse doesn't say that God suddenly put a well of water there. Nor does it say He miraculously caused a spring to flow up from the hard, parched desert ground (although He very well could have done such things). It says "God opened her eyes" and she saw something that was perhaps already there, but she hadn't yet noticed.

Maybe you're in a situation right now that looks hopeless. Maybe you're feeling like you don't have the strength to keep on parenting alone. Maybe you, too, are in a desert like Hagar and there appears to be no provision, no hope, and no guarantee that you and your children will have your needs met. It's in those kinds of situations that "the God who sees" can help us to see what we might not have noticed before. Perhaps God will "open your eyes" to the well of water nearby—the well of provision. Throughout God's Word we find promises that He will provide for us. Here are some of the wells of water that are nearby, that perhaps God will open *your* eyes to see:

1. *He provides your food.* The psalmist tells us, "I have never seen the righteous forsaken or their children begging bread" (Psalm 37:25). Do you believe that? My college youth pastor reminded me of that verse when Hugh and I were getting ready to marry and we had little income to live on in expensive Southern California. Pastor Tom always repeated that same old phrase: "The righteous will never beg bread." And to this day I've seen it's true. Why? Because the righteous are living by faith and God rewards faith;[2] because the righteous trust God and God always provides for our needs;[3] because the righteous are within the church and God often uses the church

to provide; because the righteous are blessed, and God has a "store-house" of blessings waiting for His children.

2. *He provides for your needs.* In Philippians 4:19, the apostle Paul says, "My God will meet all your needs according to his riches in Christ Jesus." How rich is He? He owns the cattle on a thousand hills, for starters. He is heir to all that is in heaven and on earth. Talk about power in high places! He's the One to be connected to. So when He says you'll have it, you'll have it.

Jesus told His followers not to worry about what they would eat or drink or wear, but to seek His kingdom first and His righteous-ness, and then all the other things would fall into place (Matthew 6:33). Having lived on a pastor's salary for more than 20 years, I can tell you that these promises absolutely hold true and God still has a way today of taking nothing and turning it into something, of mak-ing that bag of groceries mysteriously appear on the front porch, of causing that tax bill to be paid, or a debt to be erased, in a way we never expected. This is God we're dealing with. Is anything too diffi-cult for Him? (see Genesis 18:14).

3. *He provides comfort.* Our God is described in 2 Corinthians 1:3-4 as the "Father of compassion and the God of all comfort who comforts us in all our troubles." Have you dipped into His well of comfort lately? Have you sensed the peace He places on your heart that comes from knowing He will keep and protect your children? In the Bible we're told that we have a God who sympathizes with what we are going through because He, Himself, was exposed to a life of uncomfortable, trying, and often dire circumstances.[4] And because Jesus' mother, Mary, appears to have been a single parent through most of Jesus' teenage through adult years,[5] I believe He has a special heart toward single moms.

So tell me, what well of provision does God need to point out to you? Will you let Him open your eyes to it? Will you then dip from it and trust that it will always produce and never come up empty?

In Psalm 65:9, we are told that the stream of God is full of water. I believe that holds true for God's well, too. There will always be enough food, enough provisions, enough money, enough comfort, enough for whatever it is that you need.

Desiree has found God's well to be enough on days when she is weary and thirsty: "Some days are really lonely. It's also frustrating being the only adult in charge of children when there's homework to be done and doctor appointments and all the other responsibilities that go along with parenting. But the peace that I have in my spirit and the joy of my salvation and the hope in my heart of a better tomorrow and all the promises in God's Word are sufficient to meet my needs. I love that His mercies are new every morning, because I need every one of them."

God Cares for Our Children

At the end of Hagar and Ishmael's story, we're told that "God was with the boy as he grew up" (Genesis 21:20). That, I believe, can be a very real comfort to mothers who believe they carry the spiritual torch for their families, mothers who have to work and can't be there for their children as often as they wish, or mothers who must entrust their children to God in the absence of a father's role model and care.

That is reassuring to Desiree today. Recently she told me, "I used to believe that my family's spiritual well-being depended solely on me and how well I was doing spiritually. I felt that if I wasn't praying enough for my children, things wouldn't go well. I have since learned that every man, woman, and child is responsible to God for his own spiritual walk. And as far as my children are concerned, I can only do my part to the best of my abilities and trust God with the rest... and I can't make up for what they haven't received from their father."

Desiree can't, but God can. He can more than make up for it. As we learned earlier, He says in His Word that He will be "a father to the fatherless, a defender of widows" (Psalm 68:5). If that isn't care at its best, I don't know what is.

Desiree is trusting in that promise... that because there is no longer a father in the home, her children will be influenced by their *heavenly* Father instead. And as you train up your child in the way he or she should go, you can have the confidence that as they turn to the Lord and receive within them a new nature, they have more of a potential within them to be like Jesus than to be like their parents. In the words of theologian Lewis Sperry Chafer, "The new divine nature is more deeply implanted in [their] being than the human nature of [their] earthly father or mother."[6] Do your best to plant in your children a love for Jesus, and then commit the rest to their heavenly Father.

Time to Trust

Even when we go to God's well of provision and partner with Him as a parent, we will still have those days when we face difficult circumstances. But keep in mind, my friend, that it's all about fixing our eyes on the One who can take any situation in our lives and turn it into a strength.

A frustrated wife and mother of three recently wrote the following words in an email to a friend about the emotional roller coaster that life tends to be as she "does the mommy thing" alone:

> Oh Lord, use this time to make me like you because I pretty much hate it. Do I have to like it to have a good attitude? It is much easier these days, but I am weary of being home with the kids so much and all the cleaning, feeding, and everything else. On an upnote, I am very thirsty for God and for His touch in my life. That's good, isn't it? I'm sick of me, but more in awe of Him.

That precious wife and mother is about to dip into the well of God's provision—the well of thirsting for Him and finding Him— and finding that He is enough.

What about you? Are you weary, too, of doing the "mommy thing" alone? Are you like Hagar, in the desert, feeling alone as a parent with little or no hope? Do you fantasize about getting up and leaving the situation altogether because you feel you're not getting the help you need?

Remember Hagar—a woman much loved, a woman whose child

was cared for, a woman who had not escaped the notice of a loving God.

And remember "the God who sees."

You have a "God who sees" as well.

Partnering with God as a Parent

For Personal Application

1. To improve your focus on what you have in Christ Jesus, read Hebrews 12:1-3 and do the following:

   a. Identify what hinders you from persevering as a parent. Is it attitude, perspective, regrets, bitterness? If you aren't sure, ask a friend who knows you well…and be open to what she has to say. Then bring that to Jesus' feet and ask Him to rid your life of it.

   b. Pray about any sin in your life that might be entangling you and keeping you from being an effective—and joyful—parent. Ask God to point it out to you, confess it to Him, and then receive His forgiveness and strength to begin anew.

   c. Ask yourself what would be required in running the race of parenting with perseverance. Maybe you need some good "running shoes" like a support group of other single moms or a Bible study on parenting. Or, you could get together with other moms and read and review Stormie Omartian's *The Power of a Praying Parent* (Eugene, OR: Harvest House Publishers, 1995). Another idea is to inquire about a "Moms In Prayer International" group in your area (in which moms meet weekly to pray for their children who are attending school) by calling

1-800-949-MOMS or logging on to the organization's website at www.MomsInPrayer.org.

d. Worship…by praying, singing, listing all the ways you are grateful to God for what He has given you. Worship gets your eyes off of you and your circumstances and fixes them on Jesus.

2. Tape a note to your mirror, find a pretty picture of a waterfall, or buy a pretty cup to remind you to go to God's well daily and drink of what He has in store for you.

3. Find another woman who walks alone as a parent and encourage her with your story, your strength, and the well of provision that God has opened your eyes to see. As you encourage other moms who walk alone, you, too, will be encouraged.

For Further Study

Make a list of your concerns as a mother, with regard to your child or children. (These can be physical, material, emotional, and/or spiritual concerns.)

Now read the following verses and note next to each one how God provides. Then circle the ones that speak the most to the concerns on your heart:

Matthew 6:31:33:

Luke 12:22-31:

Philippians 4:6-7:

Philippians 4:13:

Philippians 4:19:

Psalm 37:25:

Proverbs 22:6:

Jeremiah 29:11:

Romans 8:28:

Spend some time in prayer thanking God for partnering with you in parenting your child or children, and for being able to take care of all the concerns on your heart. Remember, your heavenly Father loves your children even more than you do. He always knows what is best for them—and for you.

PART TWO

A Season of
Strengthening

*"The Sovereign L*ORD *is my strength; he makes
my feet like the feet of a deer, he enables me
to go on the heights."*

—HABAKKUK 3:19

Alone in Your Pain:
RELEASING THE BURDEN

Jocelyn never wanted to keep the pain locked deep inside, but she felt she had no choice. She had cried out to God, so many times, confessing to Him the things that marred her past. She knew by now that God had forgiven her. But she had a hard time forgiving herself. Jocelyn felt she couldn't share her pain—or her regrets of her past actions—with anyone else.

What will people say if they find out I was one of those women who used abortion as a form of birth control? she thought. *They will look at me differently; they will be disgusted with me. They will reject me. And I will feel the guilt and shame all over again.*

While Jocelyn knew that God was "close to the brokenhearted and saves those who are crushed in spirit" (Psalm 34:18), she felt she truly was crushed in spirit—doubled over with the pain of regrets and the wounds of shame. If God had forgiven her, why couldn't she forgive herself? Somehow there had to be a way to come out from the dark cave of feeling alone in her pain.

Jocelyn walked alone in her secret for several years, feeling she wasn't worthy of the one child God had given her that she had kept. She constantly feared God would take him away from her or, worse yet, that her son would never come to know a saving relationship with

God—all because of her past sins. But God, through the years, began showing Jocelyn that His forgiveness of her—from the moment she asked—was complete. And her next step was to forgive herself.

Jocelyn's first confirmation came the day she was confronted by her son, then 12, who asked if what his father told him about her past abortions was true. By that time, Jocelyn was vocal and passionate about protecting the unborn. *What a hypocrite I'll be in his eyes when he finds out I have done the very thing I speak out against,* she thought as she prepared to tell her son the truth. But as she admitted and apologized to her son for what she did years ago, he interrupted her and said, "It's all right, Mom. God has already forgiven you, and I forgive you, too." Jocelyn believed God was reaffirming to her His grace and forgiveness through her son's words that day. That helped her begin walking the road to forgiving herself.

But telling God—and her son—was one thing. Telling other people—especially the women in her church—was quite another! To protect herself, she decided she would continue to keep that part of her life hidden. But she found that when she, like David in Psalm 32, kept silent, her "bones wasted away" and her spirit groaned within her. She felt God's hand heavy upon her (Psalm 32:3-4).

"Not only was I hiding a dirty little secret, but I wasn't allowing God to fulfill His promise that He can use anything for His glory," she said. Jocelyn began to realize that because she wasn't sharing her story, she was keeping others from benefiting from God's grace in her life. She came to see that she could be more effective in ministering to others by talking about the grace that had lifted her up from where she had been. So, confiding in the leaders of her church's women's ministry, Jocelyn expressed a desire to begin looking for a way to funnel her pain into a source of encouragement for other women.

She received that opportunity shortly thereafter. She was asked to share her story of faith in front of nearly 200 women at her church's annual Spring event. At first, she thought, she would just tell part of the story of how God's grace found her, leaving out the more shameful details to protect herself. But the Spirit of God convicted her, and she realized that if she wanted to tell of the grace of God in her life, she had to tell her *whole story*. If she didn't, she'd be robbing God of the glory He deserved for having pulled her out of her pit. Like David sang in the first three verses of Psalm 40, she too had "waited patiently for the LORD" who turned to her and heard her cry. He lifted her out of her pit and set her feet on a rock and gave her a "firm place to stand." He "put a new song" in her mouth *so that* "many will see and fear and put their trust in the LORD" (Psalm 40:1-3). *How could she not glorify Him for that in front of all those women, regardless of how it made* her *look*, she thought.

Fears of being rejected and looked down upon nagged at the back of Jocelyn's mind throughout the week leading up to the event, but she was determined to share just how far God's love and forgiveness had reached to grasp her in His hands.

With a mind focused on giving glory to God, Jocelyn stood before those women and shared her story. She told them of her past, where Jesus found her, and what He had done in her life, speaking of His forgiveness for her and her love for Him. "I'm that woman in Luke 7 who washed Jesus' feet with my tears and kissed His feet over and over," she told the group. "I'm the one about whom Jesus said, 'She loves much because she's been forgiven much.'"[1] Jocelyn ended her story in a song of praise about how she lives to one day, in heaven, lay a crown (and not just her tears) at the feet of Jesus. As Jocelyn spoke and sang that night, not a person in the room stirred. And when she was finished, hardly an eye in the room was dry. By sharing her pain, Jocelyn connected with some women that evening who needed to hear that God's grace could cover *their* pain and shame as well.

As Jocelyn returned to her seat, I saw a confidence sweep over her and a new woman emerge…a woman who was able to stand tall again, knowing that there is no pain that is too deep to be shared for God's glory and no sin that is too far beyond God's forgiveness.

Jocelyn walked out of that place taller than I'd ever seen her walk because she had humbled herself and God had exalted her. She had straightened up from the bondage that for so many years had weighed her down and caused her to walk hunched over in pain and shame. And her face radiated with the joy of knowing that God had worked through her words to touch hearts and change lives and minister to women that evening. By sharing her pain, she had helped in the healing of others.

Turning Hurt into Hope

Me Ra Koh was a woman who kept her pain locked up inside, too. For eight years, she wouldn't talk much of the night she was raped by someone she trusted at her Christian college campus. For years she struggled with emotional pain, depression, anger, and bitterness toward the man who had betrayed her and forcefully taken her virginity. But throughout her dark struggle, the counseling, and the prayers and the pain, Jesus gently called for her to release her pain to Him and begin to live again. Me Ra eventually answered that call and bravely wrote her story. Her book, *Beauty Restored*,[2] now offers hope and healing to victims of date rape and other women who have experienced emotional trauma and pain. Today, Me Ra is a wife and mother, and she speaks at churches, conferences, and on college campuses, offering hope to those who are still walking alone in their pain. But had Me Ra kept silent and held tightly onto her pain, she would not be helping others to know about how God can heal them.

And Lisa, who was physically abused by her husband, kept her pain hidden from her family, her friends, and her church for 13 years. Despite the ridicule and threats she received from her ex-husband and his friends and their attempts to discredit her testimony, Lisa, with the help of her church, eventually walked out of the arena of hidden pain and into a refuge of care, support, and prayer. Today she is remarried (through the grace and approval of her church) to a caring man who loves her unconditionally. And she serves in her church, sings, and speaks at women's events, sharing her testimony of grace and deliverance for those who are carrying the burden of past hurts deep in their hearts.

Not Alone After All

The more I travel and speak to women across the country, the more I'm finding that Jocelyn, Me Ra, and Lisa don't have unique stories. There are women *everywhere* who hold unimaginable pain deep inside…sometimes to protect themselves from a scarred reputation, or from being misjudged, or from retaliation of some sort. Sometimes women keep silent in their pain to protect *someone else*—such as a husband or child. Sometimes they just don't know whom they can tell.

Sadly, there are women sitting in our church congregations who are being abused in their marriages and not telling anyone for fear of retaliation from their husbands. There are pastors' wives, across the country, bearing immeasurable pain because of attacks against their husbands or the stress that ministry has put on their marriages. There are women in our own Bible studies who don't feel they can talk about their boyfriend's or husband's or children's addictions to pornography, homosexuality, alcohol, or drugs. These women who are alone in their pain walk by us at church. They stand next to us in the grocery store checkout lines. They sit across from us in the bleachers, watching their children's sporting events. You might know one of them, or actually be one of them. My encouragement to you is that if you are holding in some pain you don't feel you can share, you're not alone. And the secret to strength is that your pain can be someone else's promise of hope. Your secret pain can become your story of faith, your stairway to strength that helps you offer hope and healing to others.

Because of the journey that Jocelyn, Me Ra, and Lisa have each taken, their hearts extend toward other women who walk alone in their pain.

God's heart extends toward women who are alone in their pain, as well.

Giving It to God

God's Word tells us in Psalm 62:8 to "trust in Him at all times...pour out your hearts to Him, for God is our refuge." Why would God tell us He's a refuge when He's urging us to pour out our hearts before Him? Because He knows that when we bare our souls, we face a tremendous risk. We become extremely vulnerable when we release our pain and troubles and we often fear that this vulnerability will leave us open to attack or more pain. But God wants us to know that when we tell Him all that's on our hearts, it's completely safe...like entering a protective shelter that will shield us on all sides. And when we have visited that refuge and feel safe in it, and then gain the confidence to tell others of our pain, He can use it for His glory.

Not only does God's heart extend toward you when you feel alone in your pain, His healing hand extends toward you as well.

A Healing Hand

One day when Jesus was in the temple, He noticed a woman hunched over in pain. The story in Luke 13:10-13 tells us that the hunched-over woman "for 18 years had had a sickness caused by a spirit." We don't know what her sickness was, but we know that Jesus attributed it to Satan, for verse 16 says that "Satan has bound her for 18 long years." Perhaps it was a physical condition, like arthritis or osteoporosis. Or maybe it was emotional in nature. Maybe she had become the victim of an emotional trauma or experienced devastating losses that spiraled her downward into a pit of depression from which she couldn't even physically lift her head. Maybe it was a seed of bitterness that took hold and eventually hunched her over and debilitated her. Or maybe it was fear...that past pain would never leave or future pain would catch her. Some scholars believe it was demonic oppression that deformed her body. Whatever it was, it was something that Satan used to keep her in bondage and it consumed her to the point where she couldn't even stand up straight or lift her head. And it was something that Jesus noticed and felt compassion for.

Look at what happened next! Jesus touched her, and said those precious words "You are freed," and it gave her the strength to stand again and hold up her head.

Can you imagine being doubled over in pain and bondage for so many years and then hearing those liberating words "You are freed"? It must have been music to her ears—music that let her lift her head, music that caused her to dance again!

Maybe you can relate to being doubled over in pain...to not being able to even lift your head because of the burden you carry. Maybe it's a secret from your past that you've kept buried a long time. Maybe it's something you feel you should stuff away in order to protect someone else. Perhaps the words from Jesus—"You are freed"—are words you've longed to hear all your life. If so, Jesus— the One who made you, loves you, and lives to set you free—is the only One who really *can* set you free from emotional pain, shame, or fear. He's the only One who can free any of us to stand tall and hold our heads high.

The Healer of Our Pain

I love how David calls God in Psalm 3:3: "My glory and the One who lifts my head" (NASB). David knew much about pain that was so great it would cause him to stoop over. His life was threatened for years by King Saul, he was betrayed by people close to him, his wife Michal was taken away from him, he had to separate himself from his best friend, his newborn son died as a result of his own sin, and his heart was broken by the rebellion of his adult son, Absalom. Yet David knew that in spite of his circumstances, there was One who had the power and strength and ability to free him from his pain and lift his head.

What about you? Are you doubled over with repressed pain? The Lord can lift your head and help you stand again. Are you stooped in fear of what might happen if someone found out the secrets you hold? The Lord can free you from intimidation and help you stand again. Are you bogged down by bitterness from hurt in your past? Christ can free you from its strong, suffocating grip and help you face life again.

Here is how He lovingly does it:

He Lightens Our Load

Jesus tells all of us who are "weary and burdened" (or weighted down or stooped over) to come to Him and He will give us rest (and freedom). He pleads with us to "take my yoke upon you and learn from me, for I am gentle and humble in heart, and you will find rest for your souls. For my yoke is easy and my burden is light" (Matthew 11:28-30).

Jesus carried a burden far greater than ours when He hung on the cross to pay the penalty for our sins. So surely He can carry whatever it is that is weighing us down. At a summer conference for pastors and Bible teachers, I heard Bible teacher and author John MacArthur say so eloquently what actually happened when Jesus died for us on the cross: "On the cross, God treated Jesus as if He had personally committed every sin ever committed by every person who would ever believe—even though He committed none of it." That was a pretty heavy burden! MacArthur went on to explain that "on the cross, God treated Jesus as if He lived *our* life, so that we can be treated as if we lived *His*."[3]

Because Jesus bore our sin and guilt and pain and shame, we don't have to. In fact, because He bore it, we can now walk in innocence, righteousness, and joy.

He Lights Up Our Life with Hope

We often become depressed when we feel we have no hope in a situation. And yet, in God there *is* hope. Part of the hope is that He is working our situations for good in our lives (Romans 8:28) and that He will use what we are going through to help us minister to others.[4]

In the book of Lamentations, the prophet Jeremiah is immersed in pain and troubles and says that he would have lost all hope had he not remembered the God of hope:

> I remember my affliction and my wandering, the bitterness and the gall. I well remember them, and my soul is downcast within me. *Yet this I call to mind and therefore I have hope:* Because of the Lord's great love we are not consumed, for His compassions never fail...The Lord is good to those whose hope is in Him, the one who seeks Him; it is good to wait quietly for the salvation of the LORD (Lamentations 3:19-26, emphasis added).

David and Jeremiah were in pain, and found their hope in the Lord. Jesus offers such hope to you as well. Hold on to that hope—it will see you through.

He Lifts Our Heads

Just as Jesus touched the hunched-over woman and caused her to lift her head again, He can do the same for us. When Jocelyn shared her pain with other women, she saw how God was able to lift her up out of her pit of being alone in her pain and put her on solid ground—a place of assurance that she was being used for His glory.

God also lifts our heads by helping us laugh again, love again, and live again. In Jeremiah 31:13, we are told that God will turn our mourning into gladness. And in Psalm 30:11, David says that God has "turned my mourning into dancing." God can take whatever it is that weighs us down and give to us, in spite of it, a reason to sing and dance and rejoice.

In her book *Beauty Restored*, Me Ra Koh talks of this life-giving power of Jesus to heal even the deepest of pain: "God wanted me to know that in His light, I can see myself and you can see yourself as He sees us: beautiful, clean, whole. It isn't our beauty or achievement of freedom from pain that causes us to be so; it is the Lord's great love that restores us by *freeing* and perfecting His beauty in us."[5] She adds at the end of her book that "if all other things fail on our journey to healing we can rest assured that when we tell Him all about our feelings and needs, His love will find a way to grow within us, eventually bringing light into every hidden corner of our hearts."[6]

The Power of Perspective

How can God do such a thing? What if the pain you are holding within is something so terrible that you believe nothing good could come out of it? I know some women who have been devastated by their husbands' addiction to pornography. How could God turn such mourning into a reason to dance? By changing those women's focus and giving them strength in spite of their circumstances. Look with me at what the Bible says about God's ability to do such a thing.

In Psalm 43, the sons of Korah sing of how God is our only hope in the face of discouragement. The song was written when Israel was being oppressed by its enemies. Whatever your "enemy" might be—the shame of your past, the sin you hope to cover up, the secrets you don't feel comfortable sharing, the horrible thing that has shattered your life—here are some encouraging words:

> Send forth your light and truth, let them guide me; let them bring me to your holy mountain, to the place where you dwell. Then will I go to the altar of God, to God, my joy and my delight. I will praise you with the harp, O God, my God. Why are you downcast, O my soul? Why so disturbed within me? Put your hope in God, for I will yet praise him, my Savior and my God (Psalm 43:3-5).

In this wonderful psalm of crying out to God in pain, I find five wonderful principles that can help us through those times of feeling alone in our pain:

1. *Search for truth.* When we are hurt, or trying to protect someone else, the facts can often be distorted. We can begin to trust our feelings instead of the facts. We might feel that we are alone, feel that everyone will reject us, or feel that we are being judged when

in fact we are not. To seek light and truth is to ask God to open our eyes to what is true and right.[7] In her book *Loving God with All Your Mind*, author Elizabeth George points out that focusing on whatever is true is another way of focusing on what is *real* or whatever is right before us.[8] Not our assumptions. Not our opinions. Not our fears. Not our paranoia. But the real thing. That's the first step in searching for truth—searching for what is *real*. (For more on this, see the chapter "Act on Facts, Not Feelings" in my book *When You're Running on Empty* [Eugene, OR: Harvest House, 2006].)

2. *Seek intimacy with God.* The psalmists indicated they wanted to dwell in God's holy mountain. In other words, they were saying, "Let me live close to Your heart." As we draw closer to God, He will draw closer to us (James 4:8) and give us the confidence to live out from underneath that umbrella of secrets and fear.

3. *Surround yourself with God's people.* The psalmists spoke frequently of going to the altar, which is another way of saying they would continue with public worship. In other words, they would keep being among God's people. Cutting yourself off from others when you have something you don't feel you can share will only intensify your pain.

There are some women in my church who recently discovered the beauty and benefits of a support group. They found a refuge in a small weekly Bible study called "Healing Hurts the Heavenly Way," in which they prayed for each other, looked at God's perspective on their pain, and gathered strength together. It's amazing how these women grew in just a few short months simply because they were upheld by each other's prayers and they were aware that they had a support system around them. One woman named Debbie was particularly shy and withdrawn, unwilling at first to share anything about her pain. For a few weeks, she came and listened to the others and said nothing. Once she realized that she was not alone in her pain, she was able to open up and began focusing on encouraging others rather than dwelling on her own pain.

My friend Darian, who attends another church, said it was her weekly women's Bible study group that held her together during the midst of a painful divorce. The women in her small group helped her keep her perspective, reminded her to be grateful for what she still had, and kept her grounded in the Word of God, His promises, and His comfort. "I don't know how I would've gotten by if it weren't for their prayer and support," Darian said. "On days when I didn't feel like I could pray, I knew they were praying for me…and somehow that was enough."

Never underestimate the power of a biblical, praying support group. We all need that. And make sure you're getting good Bible teaching and worship as well. That leads me to the next point.

4. *Sing.* "I will praise you with the harp, O God, my God," the psalmist said. That was their way of worshipping God. Maybe yours is just to make a joyful noise. Singing helps us to focus on God (rather than ourselves), and when we come face-to-face with Him in worship, we will no longer be thinking of ourselves and our pain, but about Him and His glory. When Jocelyn was coming to grips with God's grace and forgiveness in her life, she would listen to certain songs that worshipped God and become consumed with His holiness rather than with the ways in which she had fallen short. She admits it took years to be able to sing certain songs like "Amazing Grace" without bursting into tears. But those tears are cleansing when it comes to releasing burdens and those tears, today, are tears not of mourning, but of joy.

True worship focuses on God, not our feelings. True worship exalts Him to the point that our problems pale in comparison to the light of His glory. When I am feeling hurt, discouraged, or misunderstood, I listen to a favorite worship song that helps me to take my thoughts off my troubles and, instead, focus them upon the Lord. I truly believe that dealing with hurt and inner pain is all about focusing on God and His glory and His character—just Him alone.

5. *Set your hope on Him.* As we focus on God and His glory, there

is hope. The psalmist asks "Why are you downcast, O my soul? Why so disturbed within me?" Then he advises himself: "Put your hope in God, for I will yet praise him." He's telling himself, "Remember who is in charge, who has the power to change things and who it's all for." And when he says, "I will yet praise Him," it's as if he were saying, "I will get through this and I will live to tell of how He saw me through."

In Exodus 15:26-27, God told His people, the Israelites, that He was *Jehovah Rapha*—"the LORD who heals." He said if they would heed His voice, do what is right in His sight, and obey His commands, He would heal them of the things that plagued other nations. After giving them that promise, God led His people to a place of rest and refreshment. If we let God be our Great Healer today, He will likewise deliver us from our plagues—the hidden pain that hunches us over—and lead us to a place of rest and refreshment. Isn't that worth setting your hope in?

Where's Your Hope?

Jocelyn set her hope in God, and she received His grace and forgiveness. And her words of wisdom ring true for us today: "The Lord will forgive you whether or not you share your secret with others. But the Lord will not be able to use it for His glory unless you are willing to be vulnerable and share it."

Can you trust Him with your burden of pain, and trust Him to use it for His glory when the time comes to share it with another? Me Ra did. And God is using her story to heal others. Lisa trusted God with her pain, and saw Him deliver her from a hell on earth to become an encourager to others. She saw Him deliver her to a new life of rest, peace, and protection.

Will *you* set your hope in God…and trust Him that when you release the pain for His glory, He will lead you to a place of rest and shade—of abundance and safety and security? Will you pour out your heart to Him and let His shoulders bear the weight of your load? Will you release your pain to Him and let Him lift your head?

Remember, He carried a heavy load that day at Calvary so you wouldn't have to. Won't you let Him carry *yours* today?

Letting God Lift Your Head

For Personal Application

1. If you struggle with pain that no one knows about, pour your heart out to God and ask Him to show you a trusted friend you can confide in. Consider seeking counseling from a well-respected pastor or women's director in a Bible-believing church.

2. Write a list of the offenses—either someone else's or your own—that have caused your pain. Release these, one by one, to Jesus, asking Him for the grace to forgive—either someone else or yourself. For more on working through the steps of forgiveness, see chapter 8 of my book *When a Woman Overcomes Life's Hurts* (Eugene, OR: Harvest House, 2012).

3. Prayerfully reflect on the following verses, considering the power of God to heal our hearts, shield us, and strengthen us: Psalm 3:3; Psalm 28:6-9; Psalm 71:20-21; and Philippians 4:13. Write down any key thoughts that occur to you as you consider these verses.

4. Find a Bible study/support group in your church or area that offers help through biblical counsel and then commit yourself to healing. The book *Lord, Heal My Hurts* by Kay Arthur (Colorado Springs: WaterBrook Multnomah, 2000) is a great study for starting the healing process.

For Further Study

Perhaps your pain is partly a result of not fully understanding the loving and forgiving nature of God. Read the following verses and note a character trait exhibited by God that causes you to trust Him when it comes to healing your heart:

Psalm 9:9-10:

Psalm 30:

Psalm 32:7:

Psalm 46:1-3:

Psalm 107:17-22:

Psalm 147:3:

5

Alone in Your Spiritual Life:
DEVELOPING A DEEPER TRUST

Have you ever dreamed of what it would be like to be "spiritually one" with someone? If you're single and hoping for a spiritual partner in life, or married but not on the same page spiritually with your husband, chances are you feel you "walk alone" in your spiritual life.

Throughout the Bible, we find women who walked alone in their spiritual quest, or couples who were on different pages, spiritually. Deborah, Israel's only female judge, was a wife as well as a prophetess. But we don't hear of her husband being around to support her or work alongside her when she commands Israel to engage in war against the Canaanites. In fact, when she tells a man named Barak to go up against the wicked nation of Canaan, Barak's wimpy reply was, "If you go with me, I will go; but if you don't go with me, I won't go." Now remember, Deborah was a prophetess and judge—a woman who was accustomed to settling verbal arguments—not Xena the warrior princess. Nevertheless, she went with Barak and conquered the Canaanites. Nowhere do we read about her husband's concerns for her, much less coming out to help save her skin. Deborah carried out her "ministry" alone.[1]

Jochebed appeared to be alone, with maybe just her daughter Miriam by her side, when she put her baby son, Moses, into a basket and set him to float on the Nile River, trusting God to care for her child who would otherwise be killed by the Egyptians. Although Jochebed was married, we don't see her standing on the riverbank with her husband next to her, or her husband's arms around her, or her husband praying with her as they watched their son float down the river. It's possible that he was at work somewhere and simply couldn't come. But whatever the case, I imagine Jochebed stood there—and prayed her heart out—alone.[2]

And Abigail, who was married to a man described as "mean and surly," listened to her heart one day and prepared provisions and took them to David, the king-elect, despite her husband's hardened heart toward helping God's anointed. We learn in the story that she was used mightily by God that day to save her whole household and prevent a small war, while her husband partied with friends.[3]

Throughout time, many women have walked alone in their spiritual journey. And today, studies show that women walk alone spiritually—perhaps more than they ever have before.

A recent study of Americans by Barna Research Online[4] showed that women, in general, are more likely than men to be born again,[5] and are 10 percent more likely to attend church on a given Sunday,[6] more likely than men to have read the Bible in the past week, and nearly twice as likely to attend a Sunday morning Bible class at church or participate in a small group than their male counterparts.[7] And in general, women pray more often than men.[8] The study also showed that women are considerably more likely than men to see a closer relationship with God as "very desirable for their future." More women than men believe their faith is very important to them and nearly 70 percent of women described themselves as "deeply spiritual," whereas only half of the men surveyed would describe themselves that way.

Charles Swindoll, the author of numerous books on everything from theology to devotionals, believes that "God has given women a unique responsiveness." In his book *Esther: A Woman of Strength and Dignity,* Swindoll states, "We men are far more closed—closed toward God and closed toward one another. But women have an openness, a warmth, a responsiveness to the things of God. Women have a desire to grow, to react, to feel, to show affection toward the things of God that is not found in the average man."[9]

I bring this up not as a negative commentary on men, but to recognize some reasons we may feel alone spiritually but often can't explain why. We feel alone when no one shares the passions of our heart. We feel alone without someone to talk about spiritual things. We feel alone when no one else understands or senses what God is doing in our lives.

On Different Pages

Linda can relate. She has been active in her church and women's ministry for more than 20 years. But she has a husband who doesn't pray with her or share her passion and enthusiasm for the Lord.

"I have felt alone because we aren't on the same page, so to speak, spiritually. We are definitely in the same book of life, but on totally different pages."

In the words of another longtime friend of mine: "It can be very lonely when you can't talk about the most exciting, fulfilling thing in your life with the person that you're supposed to be one with."

Now, I am married to a man who loves God with all his heart. In fact, he's a pastor, and has devoted his life to full-time ministry. But there are still times that I feel alone in my spiritual life. There are certain expectations I have that—when unfulfilled—make me feel I walk alone spiritually. For instance, if I had my way, my husband would pray with me on a regular schedule every morning, go through a couple's devotional book with me every evening before bed, and spend at least one day a week discussing what we're learning in our personal study of Scripture. Okay, he likes that third one, because it's more of a challenge to him. But the other two are difficult to coordinate with our diverse schedules and there are times he doesn't see the necessity for them, other than to appease his wife's romantic ideas of "spiritual oneness."

I can't help but wonder if that spiritual oneness is something that we, as women, have made unattainable because of our expectations. I mean, think about it: every one of us is different, every heart beats at a different pace, every soul has a different appetite. So can we ever truly really be "one" with another, spiritually, this side of heaven?

If you are single or married to an unbeliever, you may find yourself asking this question. If you are married to a man who just isn't as fired up about his spiritual life as you are, you too may be asking this question. In either case, I want to address this subject of walking alone in your spiritual life. But because I don't live with an unbelieving husband—or a husband who is complacent in his spiritual life—I cannot claim to understand the depths of where you may have walked and the heights to which you may have reached for hope in your life and marriage and spiritual walk. But Jennifer is a woman who has been married to an unbeliever for more than 35 years. Because she is a woman who has grown incredibly stronger through her spiritual walk alone, I asked her to share the secrets to her strength, the basis for her hope, and how she has found it possible to live *with* a man (who doesn't honor God) in a *way* that will honor God. I believe you will be encouraged. (And if you find this section doesn't relate to you, please continue reading. Chances are a woman will come to your mind who needs to be encouraged by Jennifer's story.)

Jennifer's Journey

Jennifer gave her life to Christ in the fall of her senior year in high school. Because she didn't get involved in a Bible-believing church, she spent the next 10 or 11 years going to college and traveling, with no clear direction from God's Word concerning how she should live her life. During that time she dated an unbeliever for two years and agreed to marry him. She had no idea of the seriousness of committing herself in marriage to a man who didn't share her faith.

"Serious topics about life were not a part of our conversations during the two years we dated," Jennifer said. "So it is no wonder that I was in for some rude awakenings soon after marriage!"

Now that she has been married 35-plus years to a man who "wants nothing to do with religion," she understands the truth of 2 Corinthians 6:14, which warns believers not to be "bound together with unbelievers" because "there is no fellowship between light and darkness."

"Immediately I noticed the more I loved the Lord and His Word and wanted to live for Christ, the further my husband would go in the opposite direction."

Jennifer recognized early on in her marriage that her struggle was not with her husband, but "against the rulers, against the authorities, against the powers of this dark world, and against the spiritual forces of evil in the heavenly realms" (Ephesians 6:12).

So she had to have a strategy.

"Daily, hourly, I needed to be strong in the Lord and in His mighty power, putting on the full armor of God so that I might be able to stand firm against the schemes of the devil" (Ephesians 6:10-11,13-18).

Scripture flows from Jennifer's mouth as she talks. She has literally lived on the Word of God for advice about how to stay in a marriage that is difficult simply because her heart is going toward the Lord and her husband's is not.

Like many women who are married to unbelievers or to men who don't walk with their wife spiritually, Jennifer has been tempted to leave the marriage—many times.

"During the first four years of my marriage, I thought several times about leaving," she said. "Each time I would think seriously about divorce, God would bring someone or something into my life—a special message, a sermon, a book, a comment from my mother— that would bring my heart's focus back upon God, trusting that God can bless this mess."

Jennifer took very seriously Jesus' commands to not leave her husband[10] and the scriptural instruction to stay with an unbelieving husband if he agrees to live with her,[11] and therefore determined she would stick it out at all costs.

"Since my trust in and my commitment to God went deep into my heart, I remained committed in my marriage," she said. But she admitted that it hasn't been easy.

When she was making plans again to leave the marriage two years later, a friend handed her a book[12] that directed her attention to the error of *her* ways instead of focusing on her husband and his faults and how he needed to change. That began a new stage in her life, in which she quit looking to change her husband and started focusing on allowing God to change her.

"It was during this time of studying, reading, and trusting God's Word that God removed the 'D-word' from my heart, mind, and soul, and I submitted myself and my marriage to God forever."[13]

Jennifer's Encouragement

"I began to see that God brought me into my husband's life to pray for him and for his eventual salvation through a silent ministry—right here in my home."

Jennifer's "silent ministry" is found in 1 Peter 3:1-2: "Wives, in the same way be submissive to your husbands so that, if any of them do not believe in the word, they may be won over without words by the behavior of their wives, when they see the purity and reverence of your lives."

"It became very important to me that according to God's Word, my husband is sanctified, set apart, protected, because of my faith and trust in Jesus. This gave me hope, and my hope was and is in the Lord, the God of hope."

Jennifer's encouragement to keep praying, keep serving, keep respecting her husband, and keep hoping that God will work in his heart comes from Isaiah 40:28-31:

> Do you not know? Have you not heard? The Everlasting God, the LORD, the Creator of the ends of the earth does not become weary or tired. His understanding is inscrutable. He gives strength to the weary, and to [her] who lacks might He increases power. Though youths [or wives] grow weary and tired, and vigorous young [women] stumble badly, yet those who hope in the LORD will gain new strength; they will

mount up with wings like eagles, they will run and not get
tired, they will walk and not become weary (NASB).

Jennifer has gained new strength, and many times I have seen her
mount up with wings like an eagle. She is one of the leading prayer
warriors in her church. She leads a weekly prayer group for mothers of
college students who feel the burden to pray diligently for their children. She has a servant's heart. She is constantly in the Word. And this
woman, whose life I can't imagine inside the four walls of her home,
is a beacon of light and source of encouragement to all who come in
contact with her because of the sweet spirit God has developed within
her as she has "waited on Him."

During the wait, Jennifer prays as much for her own transformation of heart as for her husband's.

"From this point forward, I have focused on God changing me and
what God wants me to be doing and how He wants me to behave—
striving to be the godly woman, wife, and mother that would please
the Lord. I began the process of dying to self (Romans 6) and sub-
mitting to God and being subject to my husband (Ephesians 5:21-33)
and I truly believe that 'unless the LORD builds the house, they labor
in vain who build it' (Psalm 127:1)."

Jennifer realizes that to try to save her husband herself is to "labor
in vain" because that work on her husband's heart will only come
from the hand of God.

"I completely trust God that even though I may not have married
the man He had intended for me, He will bless our marriage and that,
as Romans 8:28 says, He will work all things out for our good.

"I recognize our marriage is missing God's best for us. We cannot receive God's full blessings unless both my husband and I know
the Lord as our Redeeming Savior. It grieves my heart to know the
years that have been wasted because of my husband's hardened heart
and the loss of blessings God would have loved to pour down upon
our lives. However, I cannot allow the grief to consume me. I must
focus, instead, on God's faithful promise in Joel 2:25: 'I will repay you

for the years the locusts have eaten.'" Believing that God will someday restore for her what has been lost has been a constant source of encouragement to Jennifer.

"As soon as the grief begins to rise in my heart, I allow myself to experience the sadness and I give it to the Lord, asking for Him to bless me. He then helps me to completely forgive my husband just as Christ forgives me of my sins, daily washing me white as snow and restoring me to fellowship with Him."

Releasing and Trusting

Nancy has done her own grieving over Stan and his refusal to give his heart to Christ. But the day she grieved the most was the day she finally released Stan into God's hands, trusting that God may save his soul someday, and then again, may not.

"The worst time of grieving in my life was coming to terms with the fact that he is not saved and might never be," she said. "But since grieving that loss, I have experienced tremendous peace."

Nancy also knows God at a depth I have yet to fathom.

"My trust is in God, not in the hope that my husband will be saved, but in God alone. God is good. God is wise. God is sovereign. And God ultimately will save whom He will save. I must trust in that."

Of course Nancy still prays for her husband's salvation. But she prays in terms of "Your will for him, not mine."

Nancy said she doesn't think about how her life might be different if she hadn't married Stan. Rather, she is convinced that her learning to trust in God's character—through her release and surrender of her beloved husband—was part of God's sovereign plan for *her* life.

Some Wisdom for Wives

I asked Jennifer to prayerfully offer advice to women like her and Nancy, who walk alone spiritually. And her words of wisdom to wives of unbelievers apply just as well for any woman who wishes her believing husband would take his spiritual walk more seriously.

Place Your Husband in God's Hands

"Years ago," Jennifer says, "God showed me that I needed to let go of my husband, move out of God's way, and allow the Holy Spirit to work in my husband's heart" (see John 16:8-11). For many women this isn't easy, but Jennifer found it a relief. "It has been a joy to let go and much more relaxing to trust God for His victory in my husband's life. My husband's salvation is between him and God, not between my husband and me. My husband is accountable to God for his behavior and actions.

"In the early years of my marriage, I would manipulate events, situations, timing, people, everything that I could to make sure he was at the right place at the right time for him to make the right decision," Jennifer said. (We do this with our believing husbands as well, don't you think?) "It was a lot of work and very tiring, frustrating, and disappointing because he never responded the way I expected him to respond. I had expectations and goals for my husband that were not his expectations and goals, which always led to my disappointment."

Jennifer had to learn once again that when she puts her expectations in the Lord, she will never be disappointed (1 Peter 2:6).

"When I let go of my husband and put him in God's hands, he can be free to be himself and grow at his own pace."

Praise Your Husband

Philippians 4:8, which shows us the mind-set that we need to have as believers and how it affects our speech and behavior, can also apply to how to live with an unbeliever:

> Finally…whatever is true, whatever is noble, whatever is right, whatever is pure, whatever is lovely, whatever is admirable—if anything is excellent or praiseworthy—think about such things.

"God's Word reminds me to look for opportunities to praise my husband," Jennifer says, "to thank him for those times he says or does positive things. I look for ways to encourage, support, love, and respect him. I always find ways and times to say, 'I love you.' Jesus has taught me how to look for the good in my husband." Jennifer cites the Proverbs 31 woman, who does her husband "good and not evil all the days of her life" (verse 12 NASB). "I too want to always speak well of my husband and do good toward him just as Jesus would do."

Prioritize Your Husband

Jennifer has found that by placing her husband's needs first—above her own and anyone else's—she is honoring him and giving him a chance to see God through her.

"At first this was difficult; however, when I saw the pleasing behavior that came from my husband, it was a confirmation that this is what Jesus would do."

Jennifer found early on that to pursue a relationship with God often means being active in Bible study, women's events, and ministry through her church. She realized that if she wasn't careful, her husband might conclude that he was not as important to her as the church, and that might cause him to resent God and the church. To keep her spiritual life from causing conflict with her husband, Jennifer has continued to show him that although she loves God and is pursuing a relationship with God, she will not neglect her husband in the process.

"Before going out at night to a Bible study or away on a weekend retreat, I always make sure that meals are prepared, the house is in order, and the children's needs are met." There have been times when Jennifer has had to pass up an opportunity or a Bible study or a planning meeting because of the needs of her husband or the obligations at home. She's learned to do that without feelings of guilt or resentment, believing that her first obligation as a servant of God is to be obedient and submissive to her husband. She knows that God sees that her heart's desire is to please her husband, and that having such a heart will please her heavenly Husband as well.

Pray for Your Husband

Jennifer has learned what it means to pray without ceasing for her husband. Not only does she pray for his salvation, but she also prays for him in every area of his life, sometimes throughout the day and throughout their conversations and struggles.

"Sometimes even when he is talking directly at me, I am praying (silently, of course) for his attitude, tone, the content of his speech. This helps me to direct my focus on God and the Holy Spirit within my heart, helping me in the difficult situations."

Pray with Other Women

"Not being able to share my prayer life with my husband, I began to look for other women who believe in the power of prayer," Jennifer said. Thirteen years ago, she discovered Moms In Touch International (now called Moms in Prayer International), which is made up of mothers who, among other things, meet regularly to pray for the lives of their children and the schools they attend. "God brought special godly Christian women who were strong prayer warriors into my life through Moms In Touch. These women filled the void of sharing prayer that my husband could not fill."

Praying with other Christian women has blessed her life, Jennifer says, and deepened her walk with the Lord.

"Yes, I can pray passionately and fervently alone; however, there is also power in numbers. I can place my husband and my children on the mat with these other praying moms. My prayers for my husband and children are being answered, in God's time, because of the prayers and faith of my fellow praying moms and wives. It's a comfort not to have to carry the mat alone."

Every woman who lives with an unbeliever or someone who is not sharing her faith needs other women around her for support, prayer, and encouragement. Let me rephrase that: Every woman—*regardless of her situation*—needs women around her for support, prayer, and encouragement. Although my husband is very interested in spiritual things, there are still some things that only a woman can understand and talk with me about when it comes to my walk with God, and that's why it's essential that we as women have other women in our life.

A Reason to Rejoice

Like Nancy, Jennifer has seen God work changes in her life that perhaps wouldn't have come about if she were not married to an unbeliever. She has seen how God has shaped her character helping her to hold her tongue and develop a sweet spirit toward her husband in spite of hurtful comments and situations. She has been forced to rely solely on the Lord and His Holy Spirit to help her overcome pain and recognize victory. She has also found direction from God and a purpose in her life through serving the Lord as the wife of an unbeliever.

"As a wife married to an unbeliever, it is my position in Christ to live for Christ as Christ would have me to live for the sake of being an example of Him before my husband and children." Jennifer's goal? That her husband would be "won without a word" (1 Peter 3:1 NASB).

God's cultivation of Jennifer in this desert of walking alone spiritually is seen in her perspective on life and her encouragement to other women who walk alone spiritually.

"I am spiritually alone in regard to my husband; however, I am spiritually full in my relationship with Christ. I have received the full measure of His joy in my heart and the Christian women whom God has brought into my life.

"I thank God for the circumstances in my life because they have brought me closer to Him, molding me and shaping me into the woman, wife, and mother He wants me to be. Galatians 6:9 tells me not to lose heart in doing good, 'for at the proper time we will reap a harvest if we do not give up.'

"God's plan is perfect. He loved me long before I even knew him, and He knows my needs and how to bring me to a closer walk with Him. And God is not finished with me yet. I have a long way to go, and I truly believe that He is molding me and bending me to do His will through learning to love and be obedient to my husband. I look forward to the day when I become His will."

Can you say that, my friend? Can you accept that perhaps your divine appointment in life is to be the silent witness through whom God works to bring your husband to a saving relationship with Jesus or a commitment that will cause him to live more fully for Christ? When you can say that, you have become a woman who has grown stronger by walking alone spiritually.

Any Heart Can Change

I know many women have thoughts of leaving their marriages because the spiritual unity and oneness isn't there, because it's too difficult to live in both kingdoms, because it's difficult for light to dwell with darkness. I hope, if that is your case, that you will heed Jennifer's advice to stick it out—and grow stronger in the Lord, see your role as that of a silent witness in your husband's life, and gain a deeper trust in the God who can save souls and transform lives.

Robin, too, had a difficult time believing, at one time in her life, that God could save or change *anyone*. But she let me share her story to encourage you that no heart is beyond the transforming power of the Lord.

Robin believed her husband, Jack, shared her faith at the time they married. But a few years into her marriage, she realized Jack had neither a relationship with Christ nor a desire for one. He wasn't adamant against Christianity; he just didn't feel a need for religion in his life. "He was so unreachable because he was so at peace with himself and he didn't appear to need God," Robin said.

"Being a quiet and very private person, he didn't talk about what he was feeling and what was on his heart. There was a lot of silence. It was almost impossible to get through to him. He didn't know how to be a compassionate person and share the deep things on his heart or be compassionate when I shared things." That created a chasm between them that Robin believed would never be crossed.

For several years, because Robin was raising their children and Jack was working long hours, they saw little of each other and talked even less. But when Robin started attending a Bible study with other women who were praying for their unbelieving husbands, things started to change.

"I realized I needed to be growing spiritually so that my husband could see the difference that God can make in a person's life," she said. "I developed a heart relationship with God during that time that I couldn't have with my husband. I also learned how to pray for Jack, how to have a gentle and quiet spirit, and how to cultivate my own relationship with the Lord so Christlikeness flowed through me and wasn't forced."

For nearly 15 years, Robin grew in her closeness to the Lord, praying constantly that Jack's heart would open to the Lord. But nothing in her husband seemed to change. Robin remembers feeling desperate for God to do *something* in Jack's life as she leaned her head against the shower wall one day and prayed, "God, I'm tired of living in a home that is not Christ-centered. Please God, do whatever it takes to get this family where you want it. Do whatever it takes to turn Jack's heart toward you."

Robin believes the "whatever it took" came a week later, when they received some devastating news about their teenage daughter, followed shortly by their daughter's attempt to kill herself. Shaken to the core by this crisis, Robin turned to God for help. She had been studying about the character of God and immediately held on to Him as her Rock, her Provider, and her Shelter in the storm.

Jack saw that Robin had an unworldly strength during that family crisis and he wanted to possess that strength as well. When he reached out to his wife one day, wanting to comfort her, she told him the only place she could find comfort was through prayer, and she knew he couldn't possibly comprehend that or share that with her. For Jack, the knowledge that his wife had found a comfort in Someone other than him perhaps frightened him or challenged him, as he later told

Robin that those words cut him to the core and made him think about his own lack of strength and ability to be there for his wife.

The following Sunday, Jack attended church with his wife, and during the communion service, bowed his head and surrendered his life to Christ. When he told Robin about his decision that evening, they—for the first time in their married life of nearly 20 years—prayed together. They also renewed their marriage vows and dedicated each of their children to the Lord.

It has been several years since Jack's surrender to God, and Robin has seen slow, steady changes in her husband as he is gradually becoming the man God intended him to be. But when the changes don't come quick enough for Robin, she often has to keep herself from jumping in and trying to speed things up. "After being the spiritual head of our home for so long, I have to keep reminding myself to let God continue to do the work He started in Jack. It isn't up to me to get him to the place that I envision for him."

Robin often tells women who are longing for their husbands' hearts to change that God can save anyone—but He will do it in His way and His timing. "Ask God for a vision for the future [when it comes to your husband's salvation]...ask Him for hope for what things will be like someday. That is faith. That is believing in His timing and His ultimate control over the situation."

And that is believing that God can change anyone.

I remember times in my own life when I have muttered under my breath, "That person will *never* change. Not even God can change him." How ignorant—and arrogant—of me to think that anyone is beyond the transforming power of God! Some of the very people that I foolishly muttered against have since been changed from the inside out and are constant reminders to me that God's grace can extend toward *anyone*. I know now that no life is beyond God's power to transform, no heart is beyond God's ability to soften, no soul is beyond His reach to save. Not Jack's. Not your husband's. Not anyone's.

A Time to Trust

If you are concerned that your husband might never turn to God, get your expectations off of your husband. He doesn't have it in his power to desire the things of God. Scripture says none of us do (Romans 3:10-12; 8:7). It is only God's power working within us that enables *any* of us to love Him, desire Him, and want to please Him.

When you switch your focus from your husband to God, you may or may not see changes in your husband, but you'll definitely see changes in yourself. That's what Robin did. That's what Jennifer is doing. That's what God honors.

Put your hope in the One who made your husband and loves him far more than you ever could. Remember, our God desires your husband's heart even more than you do. Our God is the One who can reach your husband with His arm that is not too short to save (Isaiah 59:1). Our God is the One through whom all things are possible (Genesis 18:14). Don't say, "Even God can't change his heart!" Instead, say, "God, You are big enough to reach anyone and You are wiser than me in Your ways and Your plans. I trust You to work in ways that I can't."

And in the meantime, you *grow*, girl! God will be with you every step of the way.

Developing a Deeper Trust

For Personal Application

1. Think of ten things to praise your husband for this week (and list them here):

   Now think of at least five different ways you can express that praise to your husband. Be creative—not every element of praise needs to be verbal.

2. Write out a prayer releasing your husband to the Lord. Keep this where you will be reminded of your "sacrifice."

3. If your husband is an unbeliever, what three ways can you encourage him this week? (For some help, see my free article "What Speaks Love to Your Husband?" under the "Resources and Encouragement/Encouragement for Couples" tab at my Web site, www.StrengthForTheSoul.com.)

4. If your husband is a believer, in what ways can you encourage him spiritually this week?

5. If you are unmarried, how can you look to God to be your "spiritual encouragement" in your walk with Him? (For some help or inspiration, see a number of my free "Articles of Encouragement" under the "Resources and Encouragement" tab at my website, www.StrengthForTheSoul.com.)

For Further Study

Which Old Testament "woman who walked alone" can you most relate to, and why?

- Deborah, the strong woman who fought alone (Judges 4:1-16)
- Jochebed, the mother who said good-bye to her little son (Exodus 2:1-10)
- Abigail, the wife who honored God in spite of her husband's attitude and behavior (1 Samuel 25:1-42)

Read the story of Abigail in 1 Samuel 25:1-42.

What did Abigail do that showed wisdom as a wife?

What characteristics did she display that are worth imitating?

How did God reward her?

How can this woman be a personal encouragement to you?

Download my article "Accepting His Spirituality" from the "Encouragement for Couples" section of my website (www.StrengthForThe Soul.com) and write a one-paragraph response as to how you will accept your husband spiritually or help encourage another woman to do the same.

If you don't have a prayer circle, find at least two women who believe in the power of prayer and ask them to meet with you weekly to pray for your husband, your marriage, and your spiritual walk. Suggested Material: *The Power of a Praying Wife* by Stormie Omartian (Eugene, OR: Harvest House, 1997), *Loving Your Husband* by Cynthia Heald (Wheaton, IL: Victor Books, 1978), and *When a Woman Inspires Her Husband* (Eugene, OR: Harvest House, 2011).

Alone in Worship:
EXPERIENCING MORE OF GOD

or years, Debe longed to have Randy worship alongside her. She was tired of sitting in church alone, singing songs of praise alone, taking notes on the pastor's sermon alone. Her heart ached for her husband to experience what she did through the music and the message at church.

Because her heart was focused on her husband's need for Jesus, Debe remembers filtering every sermon through her husband's life. *Randy needs to hear that*, she would think. Or, *This verse is for Randy.*

After several years of worshipping alone, Debe became discouraged—and sometimes even depressed—that her husband was not joining her in the most important quest in her life, and she was not growing because of it. She finally decided it was time to leave the marriage so she could find someone who would share her heart, worship alongside her, and encourage her in her walk with God. But Debe's pastor talked her out of it. He encouraged her to start focusing on *her* growth with the Lord, not her husband's. As Debe began to do that, she discovered that there was a whole new side of God she never really knew before.

"Worshipping alone then took on a whole new dimension," Debe said. "The intimacy of my worship began to increase as I looked to God (and not Randy's presence beside me) to fill the longings of my heart. It became more one on one with Jesus and me. My spiritual and even emotional needs were being met during those times. In my quiet times, He led me to scriptures that were relevant to my life. Because I love music, I often spend time singing praises, and with each time of worship, my relationship with Jesus deepens. I am praying, I am listening, and I am growing."

Debe came to realize that being alone in worship could be a wonderful thing!

Rona feels alone in worship, too. Because she is unmarried, she wonders when the day will come that she will no longer feel alone when she sits in church. "What is it like to have a husband next to you who holds your hand during the service? What is it like to be able to sit in church with someone you love?" she asks.

Alone Again, Spiritually

When I married Hugh 25 years ago, I remember being very excited about the prospect of worshipping God together with my husband. I had always dreamed of the picture-perfect scene of sitting together with my husband in a newly marrieds class, going through homework together, doing devotions together every night before we went to sleep, and standing side by side or sitting hand in hand at church every Sunday, worshipping together.

To this day, that has seldom happened.

Because my husband was already teaching Bible classes before we were married, my romantic notion of taking the newly marrieds class together never panned out. In our first year of marriage, I attended the class Hugh taught on the book of 1 Peter. By the time that was over, he was teaching the college/singles group, and I helped out. Then he graduated from Bible school and got ordained as a minister and was up in the pulpit for the next eight years, while I continued to sit alone in church. (I literally sat alone because few people felt comfortable sitting in the first or second row next to the pastor's wife—that happens in churches for some odd reason!) During those years of "sitting alone" I came to realize that God could use me more if I served in some capacity, so I began teaching Bible classes, helping in the nursery, or singing on the worship team.

Nine years later, when Hugh and I took a position on staff at a larger church, we still didn't have the luxury of worshipping together. He was teaching Bible classes during one of the services, and I taught during the other. My husband and I continued to pass each other "like ships in the night" on Sunday mornings at church. And today, my husband is back in the pulpit as a senior pastor and I'm back in the front row sitting by myself, unless I can persuade someone to sit with me up there—usually a woman I find who is sitting alone. Because we've been ministering "together" all these years, my husband and I have rarely experienced "worshipping together."

There were a few times in our first few years of marriage that we did sit side by side during a *portion* of a worship service, and I recall my focus was on who was next to me, not who I was there to worship. *Why isn't he putting his arm around me like all the other husbands do with their wives in church? Will he hold my hand during prayer or is he still mad that I made him late this morning? Did he catch what the pastor said, or is he thinking that it applies to* my *life?*

I've had times when I longed for Hugh to sit next to me as I worshipped. But the day I realized that worship was not about who was—or wasn't—sitting next to me was the day I really learned to worship.

Now, I can tell you firsthand that it's actually good when we can worship alone because worship *is* something that's between us and God. And from a physical standpoint, while we might prefer to not have to worship alone, even that can be a wonderful thing for us.

Hannah's Alone Times

Hannah knew well what it meant to worship alone, pray alone, and carry burdens on her heart alone. She desperately wanted a child more than anything else on earth. And one day she bitterly poured out her heart to God about it. She told Him of her longings, her sadness at seeing all the other women around her with children, her frustration that she couldn't give her husband a child, and her sorrow at being the brunt of jokes from her husband's other wife. She prayed, cried, and told God that if He would give her a child, she would give him back to the Lord for service in the temple all his life. This woman laid it on the line with God, and she did it alone. Her husband, Elkanah, must have been in another part of the temple worshipping and offering his sacrifices. But Elkanah didn't need to be with Hannah. God met Hannah there as she prayed and worshipped alone. And He gave her that child she prayed for.

After weaning her son, Hannah again went to the temple, but this time she went to praise God for His gift to her and to leave her son with the priest. And she appeared to do that alone, as well. Do you ever wonder why she didn't ask her husband, Elkanah, to pray with her for her child? Do you find it odd that it's a mother's prayer and song of praise that is recorded in 1 Samuel 2 and not one that is shared by the father, too? I tend to think that Hannah had such a deeply personal experience with God when she begged for a child that she wanted to be alone when she went back to God again. In her earlier visit to the temple, she had some "pouring out" to do and she wanted to do it alone. Later, after being given a child, she had some praising to do, and she wanted to do that alone. It was personal—between her and God. And it didn't matter to her, apparently, whether or not a man or someone else was beside her. What counted most to her was that God be praised.

Alone in Prayer

My friend Sara can relate. When I asked her if she—like so many other women—ever felt alone in prayer, perhaps from not having a husband who prayed with her regularly, her response took me by surprise. "Oh, Kurt does pray with me when I ask him to, but why would I want anyone else in the room when I'm pouring my heart out to God?" she said. "Prayer is such a deeply personal thing between me and God, and I treasure those times alone with Him." Granted, Sara's response gave me a glimpse into the depth and intensity of her prayer life. And it also reminded me that prayer—like worship—is often an alone thing, too. After all, it's much easier to pray to God from the deepest depths of our hearts when we're alone.

Now Sara's response, I think, is unusual. Most women I've met complain about, rather than relish, being alone in prayer. Many women—including several pastors' wives—have told me that it's like splitting hairs to get their husbands to pray with them. Many of them have praying husbands, but their husbands pray on their own. That's been true as well for my husband, who for years had his devotional time early in the morning before I got up. I had my time alone with God after he left the house. We each prayed, but had difficulty finding the time to do that together—just the two of us. It is a continual challenge today to make that time to pray together on occasion, but because of our circumstances, for the most part, I have had to pray alone.

For several years this bothered me. And I imagine when some women read that my husband and I don't pray together daily at a regularly scheduled time—just the two of us—it might bother them as well. After all, how can we be qualified for ministry if we aren't of "one mind" in prayer? And yet, God in His grace, has a way of making Hugh and me of the same mind by working on us individually. And we've experienced plenty of times when we've been of one mind because God had worked in each of our minds and spirits, and not because we heard each other praying about certain things.

Now, don't get me wrong. I would still love to have that opportunity in my day—every day, or even once a week!—to pray with my husband. And now that our daughter is grown and we're in a different season of life, it is much easier. But God is showing me that to come to Him alone should always be a priority, no matter what the situation and no matter who comes along. And when the time comes that my husband and I can schedule time together to pray—every day—that will be the icing on the cake!

Do you need to focus solely on God right now and not whether or not your husband—or someone else—is joining you in prayer and worship?

Becoming a Worshipper

Shortly before writing this book, as I was studying the life of Abraham (who was called "the friend of God"), I read that "Abraham was supremely a worshipper, and his life is a testimony to this fact."[1] That prompted me to ask myself, "Am *I* supremely a worshipper? Is *my* life a testimony to that fact?"

I used to think that worship was something I did in church when the music played, but the definition of worship is "a deliberate, steady, focused time with God...Worship is totally God-centered...God-focused."[2] Although it may sound romantic and even more spiritual to "worship together" with a husband, true worship happens when there is only one person on my mind and in my heart—the Lord Jesus. Oftentimes, when I'm busy in ministry, that deliberate focus doesn't even happen on a Sunday morning at church! Worship, then, is anytime I go out alone with God—either physically or in my mind and spirit—and focus on Him and Him alone. That definition (and that statement about Abraham) stirred up a hunger in my heart to know more of what it means to truly worship God. So I went to the Bible's worship center—the book of Psalms—to look at examples of praise and worship.

Worship Is Personal

As I looked through the Bible's "song book," what impressed me most is that out of 150 songs of praise, 90 of them were written from a personal perspective, recounting a personal experience with God. Only about 25 of the songs referred to corporate worship, using the terms "us" and "we." This seems to indicate that much of worship takes place as a personal encounter with God. While we are to not forsake assembling together with other believers for corporate worship (Hebrews 10:25), we can't live off of church worship services as our extent of worshipping God. Worship must also flow from our personal lives, and much of that flow will happen when we are alone. Much of worship is an alone thing.

Look with me at an example of worship flowing from a person's alone times with God. In Psalm 18, David sang:

> I love You, O LORD, my strength. The LORD is my rock, my fortress and my deliverer; my God is my rock, in whom I take refuge. He is my shield and the horn of my salvation, my stronghold (verses 1-2).

Look at how very personal that song is. David sings to God so intimately, calling him *my* rock, *my* fortress, *my* deliverer, *my* God, *my* shield, *my* salvation and *my* stronghold.

As you read about David's life in other portions of the Bible, you can see how he experienced firsthand the Lord as his rock, fortress, deliverer, shield, salvation, and stronghold. David can worship God because of his *personal experience* with God. David can worship God alone…because of the times he has encountered God alone.

In verses 3-6 of that song, David recalls how he called to the Lord and how the Lord heard his voice. Then in verses 7-15, he describes God's thunderous response to save the one who called upon Him. And in verses 16-19, David describes God's tender rescue of him in the midst of his troubles:

> He reached down from on high and took hold of me; he drew me out of deep waters. He rescued me from my powerful enemy, from my foes, who were too strong for me. They confronted me in the day of my disaster, but the Lord was my support. He brought me out into a spacious place, he rescued me because he delighted in me.

David's experiences with God can't be separated from his worship of God. They are intertwined. So it should be in our lives as well.

Worship Is Passionate

Because of the intensity of David's personal experience with God, worship and praise flowed from his heart. It was natural, at that point, for David to be consumed with praise for this God who had proven

Himself God in David's life. As David became passionate for God, so David praised God. In Psalm 27:4, David expresses the passion of his heart by saying there is *one thing* he wants more than anything in life: to "dwell in the house of the LORD…to gaze upon the beauty of the LORD and to seek him in his temple." David is saying he wants nothing more than to get up close and personal with God. He wants nothing more than to worship God face-to-face. Did you catch that? He wants *nothing* more. He doesn't need anyone else around him to worship (not Michal, his first wife. Not Abigail, his second wife. Not all his children, not his best friends or his servants or his mentors). He doesn't need any *thing* around him, such as the right type of music or atmosphere. He only wants to be in God's presence, worshipping Him. In other words, if it's just him and God, it's enough. Oh, if we could just say that as well!

As we begin to desire God more than anything else, we can't help but worship Him. And as we worship Him, we can't help but desire Him. Passion for God and worship of God go hand in hand.

Worship Prepares Our Hearts to Hear God

As we set aside ourselves and focus on God, we can discover more of who He is as He reveals Himself to our worshipping heart. It's interesting to note that many of the Psalms begin with the songwriter talking of distresses. But then the writer focuses on God, gets a new perspective, and ends his song in praise. It's as if these writers experienced change *while* they were singing to God. That's one of the incredible things about worshipping God without the distraction of others: He often reveals who He is and what He wants to do with our lives.

I had this experience several years ago. As I was asking God to clarify some of the plans He had for my life, I felt Him tugging at my heart to go away alone with Him. Since my husband was out of the country at the time and there wasn't a chance he'd call and need anything, and my daughter was in school for another couple hours, I answered the call. Now, I didn't have the time to go away with God.

I had several more chapters in this book to write, and the deadline was rapidly approaching. I also had a dozen phone calls I needed to make and letters I needed to send for my church's women's ministry. But God was calling, "Come away with Me." So I went to the nearest remote place that I could find—a community lake at the base of a mountain called Double Peak (in San Marcos, California). As I climbed the three-mile hike up Double Peak, I was determined to focus on God during that time, not all the "noise" in my head. I looked around at all that He had created, closed my eyes, listened to the birds, and remembered how He promised in His Word to care for me,[3] and I praised Him for who He is.

As I was climbing, I also thought about how much higher this mountain was and how much longer it took to climb than the hill behind my old home in Sun City, California, where I used to climb for my devotional walks. It was then that I realized why God had summoned me up to this mountain. About nine months earlier, when I had left my high-desert home to come live in San Marcos, I was saddened that there weren't any mountains for me to climb near my new home. But I realized on this hike that God had not only given me another mountain to climb, but a higher one, and one that took a lot more endurance to climb. And when I reached the top, I realized He'd given me a mountain upon which I could see a lot more than I could atop the one back home. I had been praying for several months for God to expand my territory of influence in ministry, and by the time I got to the top of Double Peak, I could see that He had. God had enlarged my view and increased my area of influence. He had given me a bigger challenge, a tougher climb, but one that reaped greater rewards. I stood on that mountaintop soaking in the cool breeze that swirled around me and feeling amazed at the love that drew me there to show me who He was and what He was doing in my life.

God sometimes chooses to reveal Himself and His plans to us when we get alone to worship Him. If I had climbed that mountain with someone else that day, we might've talked the whole way—perhaps about what God is doing in our lives. But I probably wouldn't have heard anything from God Himself. That's why the worship times alone can be so fruitful.

Worshipping with Others

As important as it is to seek God's face without the distraction of others, I want to be careful to not imply that we can worship and maintain a relationship with God apart from the presence and participation of others. In the Bible, we repeatedly see people coming together to worship God in corporate prayer and singing. And in the book of Revelation, we are told that someday, together with all the saints who ever lived, we will encircle the throne of God and worship Him together. And, as I mentioned earlier, we are told in Scripture not to forsake assembling together for worship while we're still here on earth (Hebrews 10:25).

Many of us learn to pray by hearing the prayers of others. Many of us learn to worship by watching or worshipping with others. But we must be careful not to *depend* on others when it comes to worship and prayer. We want to be able to worship God just as fully by ourselves as when we are surrounded by others.

Depending on God, Not Others

My friend Tammy remembers a time in her life (during her first marriage and subsequent relationships) when she hung on to the spiritual coattails of the man in her life. If he wanted her and the children to go to a certain church and not another, that's what they would do. If he wanted to sleep in one Sunday and just skip church altogether, that's what they'd do. It also meant that if he had no desire to worship or pursue the things of God, she, too, would follow his lead. But she was also miserable in those relationships.

"I recognize that all of my struggles that occurred early in life were because I allowed myself to ride the spiritual wave of the man in my life," Tammy said.

Tammy is now in her second marriage and has come to see that her spiritual experience is all about her personal relationship with God, not her relationship with a man. Because of that new perspective, her life has taken a whole new turn. This woman who once showed no initiative spiritually is now one of the most driven women I know when it comes to pursuing her relationship with God. She is in more small-group Bible studies than any other woman I know, she is heading up her church's ministry to moms, she supervises a kids' club for young mothers in the community, she is discipling younger women in the faith, and she is actively raising her children in the knowledge of the Lord.

And, every Sunday, Tammy, bless her heart, worships alone. Not because her husband is at home, but because he's on the platform, accompanying the worship team on the keyboard. Tammy has gone from being alone in worship (because she had no one to encourage her spiritually) to being alone in worship (because of the ministry demands on her husband). But through all of that, she has learned that worship happens not when her husband sits beside her and encourages her to sing, not when her whole family is together or at peace with each other, not when things are right in her life externally, not when the songs are familiar to her, but when she is in God's presence and meets Him face-to-face. Just Tammy and God. And it is real. It is personal. And I believe Tammy would tell you, it is precious.

What about you? Can you see being alone in worship as something precious, too? Can you recount the personal experiences you have had with a powerful yet patient, thundering yet gentle, all-knowing and all-forgiving God and then just pour out your heart in praise to Him whenever you get the chance? Sometimes I don't have to reflect on past personal experiences with God in order to start praising Him; sometimes it's enough just to focus on Him, and then the praise flows.

Worship as a Way of Life

My most meaningful times of worship (the times I've forgotten about myself and just focused on God) have sometimes been as simple as taking an old hymn book off of the shelf in my study and turning to a song like "Praise to the Lord the Almighty" and singing it. Other times, it's nothing more than quietly reflecting on who He is: Creator, Sustainer, Holy One, Savior of Mankind, Lord of all there is.

Sometimes we have to be creative in how we worship Him alone. I have found that I will starve my soul if I try to live all week long on just 20 minutes of worship during a church service every Sunday. Any of us will, if that's the only time we focus deliberately on God and sing praises to Him. So I have tried to carve out niches of time every day during which I endeavor to give honor to God and grow in the skill of worshipping Him. (I say *skill* because in my life, worshipping God is not something that comes naturally. Worshipping self or people or things comes naturally. Therefore I must set aside time to learn to do that which God requires of me, and that which I now want to do for Him.) I've found that setting time aside for worship is essential if I want to be a person who, like Abraham, is supremely a worshipper.

God's Word isn't vague about how we are to worship the Lord. The Bible gives clear guidelines for worshipping Him, and we can incorporate these into our times alone with God:

1. Worship Him with humility. Psalm 95:6 says, "Come, let us bow down in worship." In every scriptural encounter between man and God, we find the man on his face. He is bowed over, face to the floor, in humility and fear and awe. To humble ourselves is to forget about us and focus on Him. That day atop Double Peak, I had an urge within me to sing loudly to the Lord. But I couldn't tell if someone might walk around the bend and hear me…that would have been embarrassing! But then I figured, *Worship is about Him, not me or how I sound or look to anyone else.* So I sang—to the rocks and trees and the wide open air that descended beneath me.

We can worship in humility by bowing our heads, by getting on our knees, by lowering ourselves before the throne. In my own prayer and worship time, getting on my knees does something to my heart; it makes me realize that I am nothing and He is everything—the first step in recognizing His worth and worshipping Him.

2. Worship Him with gladness. Psalm 100:2 says to worship God with gladness and "joyful songs"—songs that bubble up and flow out of our hearts because we love Him. I sing best when I'm by myself, when only His ears hear me. What about you? Can you sing to God, as an expression of gladness when you are alone? How about being glad simply because He is God and you have been given the great privilege of knowing Him?

3. Worship Him from the heart. I recently spoke at a large women's gathering in which the women were asked to sing "I Love You, Lord" before I spoke. The song speaks of lifting our voices to worship God as our soul rejoices. After the first time through, I looked around at the women who were singing. Because I was speaking on reflecting the light of the Lord in our lives and showing His joy in our faces, I wanted to see their faces as the song was being sung. These women knew the song well enough to sing it without reading the words— but it was difficult to tell where their hearts were as they sang. Many of them were looking around, looking through their purses, or looking straight ahead at the women leading the song. From their faces, I couldn't tell they were in love with God or that they were rejoicing. That made me think of the times I've sung to God, but my heart was not really worshipping Him.

In Matthew 15:9 Jesus revealed what He thought about people worshipping Him when their hearts were not engaged. He warned about "people [who] honor me with their lips but their hearts are far from me." He said, "They worship me in vain."

When I'm honest with myself, I can recall times that my worship of God has been in vain because someone or something else— other than Him—was on my mind.

If, in worship, God requires all of our heart and all of our focus, then what better way can we do that than when we are all alone? It's possible to be surrounded by other women at a table or have a man at our side or a child in our lap and still enter God's presence alone. It all depends on who we take with us in our minds and hearts...someone else, or the Lord alone.

Going Away with Him

God is not limited in how He speaks to us, ministers to us, or provides for us. Nor is He limited in how He will receive our worship. So get out of the box. Take a worship walk and praise Him as you go. Climb a mountain and talk to Him along the way. Sit in your living room, listening to worship music. Take out your Bible and read aloud the names of God. Sit outside on your porch, by your garden, or on a park bench and breathe in the beauty of His creation and let every sense that you have respond in loving praise to the Creator. Focus on Him and His greatness...and you'll be worshipping Him.

I love what Jesus said to a group of religious leaders who were upset that the noise level got a little loud when people were praising Him: "If they keep quiet, the stones will cry out" (Luke 19:40). I believe Jesus was saying that all creation was meant to worship Him. So if everything He made is bursting with reason to praise Him, we who have been given voices to do so must lead the throng! My friend, use any chance you get alone to praise Him. If you're waiting for a bus, praise Him. If you're in your car waiting to pick up a child, worship Him. If you're driving down the street and you hear something that reminds you of Him, sing out your praises. If you're walking the beach or standing in line at the post office, close your eyes and remember the One to whom praise is due. It doesn't matter what the rest of the world thinks. Worship is between you and God.

There are times in my life when I feel that need to "go away" with God. I think that tugging on my heart is God's way of saying, "Cindi, it's been a while. Come away with Me so we can have some time together." It amazes me that God, who cares for the entire universe, desires to spend time alone with us. So when He calls, I go, thankful that He has noticed how time has slipped away and that I need to be back at His side.

Has God been calling you? Or have you been too preoccupied with the people—or lack of people—sharing your worship experience with you to hear His call? Will you wait for His gentle tug on your heart to go away with Him, or will you seek Him now, right there where you are, as a way of saying, "God, I am alone here…but I know this is where You want me so You can get up close and personal with me—so You can receive my worship of You. Be worshipped, Lord Jesus, for You are worthy."

"Holy, holy, holy is the Lord God Almighty, who was, and is, and is to come" (Revelation 4:8). That's the song we will sing around the throne of Christ someday in heaven. So, won't you begin practicing it now…so that those words become your passion?

Shifting Our Focus

When I switched my focus from who was sitting next to me and onto who was above me, worship became a much more fulfilling experience—to the point that God's presence alone was what I longed for. As long as I keep my gaze heavenward, I don't feel as if I'm all alone in my worship.

My friend, do you feel alone when you worship God? Then be encouraged with this: There is no other way to worship! When the distractions are behind you and the other people in your life have dwindled in significance, it's much easier to see the Lord. And whether you are alone at church, at home, in your car, or in your bed, you can worship the Lord. And when you do, may it bring joy to your heart just to know that you are *not* alone. You are in the presence of the Almighty…and He's been waiting for a chance to be alone with *you*.

Deepening Your Experience with God

For Personal Application

1. Take some time now—or as soon as possible—to spend time in the presence of the Lord. Here are some suggestions for that time:

   a. Listen to some worship music, close your eyes, and dwell on the presence of God.

   b. Read some Psalms aloud (try Psalms 8, 29, 46, 96, or 150), or better yet, sing them! They were each written to music, so guess at the tune. There may be several that you recognize from a tune someone has written for them.

   c. Write a song of praise that describes who God is, what He's done for you, and your response.

2. Take a worship walk and praise God in everything you see, feel, and experience.

3. Make a list of the names by which you have come to know God personally (for example, Lover of my soul, Provider, Protector, Defender, Light of my life, and so on). Then read this list back to God as a form of worship.

4. Set some goals for yourself in terms of worship. For example, how much time a week or month do you want to devote to worship? How will you hold yourself accountable? What good books do you want to read on the subject of worship? How will you know if you are gradually becoming "a worshipper"? (And if you struggle with finding time to set aside for worship, see my book *When Women Long for Rest* [Eugene, OR: Harvest House, 2004] as a training course in taking the time to sit at God's feet and worship Him.)

For Further Study

Read the following portions of Scripture out loud and worship the Lord by writing a one-sentence response next to each passage, praising Him for who He is or what He has done.

Job 42:2:

Psalm 8:1,3-6:

Psalm 13:5-6:

Psalm 16:2:

Psalm 63:3:

Psalm 73:25-26:

Psalm 95:3-5:

Psalm 100:5:

Ephesians 3:20-21:

Alone in Your Trials:
FINDING YOUR GLORY STORY

*E*rin felt like her life was falling apart.

"I just don't understand it," she said. "It's been one slam after another for the past ten years...actually, for my whole life." Although Erin appeared on the surface to have everything—a successful career and ministry, a lot of friends, a high self-esteem—she recounted to me the pain in her childhood, the string of broken relationships over the past several years, her kidney disease, the repeated sicknesses, the hospitalization from a nervous breakdown, the decline of her business, the eviction from her home, her broken marriage engagement, and now her diagnosis of cancer.

"Each time I get slammed against the wall, I pick myself up, dust myself off, and move on. I pray about it constantly and ask God to show me the lessons He wants me to learn. And still this keeps happening. What's wrong with me? Am I doing something wrong?" she asked as the tears began to fall. "When is enough, enough?"

I sat across the table from Erin not knowing what to say. The words of wisdom I had hoped for wouldn't come. The Scripture verses I'd memorized for situations like this seemed rote and cliché at the moment. Erin was broken...and there was nothing I could do to fix her.

As I watched the tears stream down her cheeks, I thought about how helpless she looked at this moment and how unlikely a picture it appeared to be. This self-reliant, strong-willed, determined, and very confident woman was finally broken. Could it be that she was now at the point where God could rebuild her from the ground up and make her a *God*-reliant, flexible, focused, and confident woman in Him?

I managed a whisper as I reached across the table and squeezed Erin's hand: "Sounds like God is writing quite a glory story."

As I drove home in silence, I thought about the "glory story" God writes on the fabric of our lives. I thought about the underside of that tapestry, where all the knots and imperfections are, so that the top side can be perfect and intricately beautiful. I thought of this God who has a way of weaving lessons and revelations of His love into the troubles that bombard us in life. And when we are determined to see that He gets the glory for all that we encounter, then the things we go through are not for nothing.

Erin's story wasn't finished. In fact, it was just starting. And a few weeks later when I talked to her on the phone, she sounded much more upbeat. "I think I know why all this is happening to me," she said. "I don't really *know* God. All this time I've been praying to Him and serving Him, but I didn't really know His character and the full aspect of who He is. Now through the chemotherapy, through the crying out to Him every day, through the way I've been searching His Word for answers, I am finally getting to *know* Him. I think, for the first time in my life, I'm really *experiencing* Him." Erin may not have realized it, but right there on the phone she was already recounting God's glory story in her life.

Within a few months of that conversation with Erin, she connected with an agent who helped her get her first book written and published. About a year after that, she had found and married the love of her life. Then she was given a prestigious title in her community for her volunteer work in the crusade against breast cancer. A few months later, she spoke at my church, giving her testimony and glory to God for all He had done in her life.

Since that original conversation with Erin and watching what God did afterward, I've thought many times about God's glory story as I've listened to women describe their trials in life and the way they walk through situations alone. And in all the stories, I'm convinced that even though life might look at times like it's spinning out of control, there's a God who knows what He's doing. He's weaving a lesson, preparing a promise, readying a revelation of Himself…He's writing His glory story.

Job's Glory Story

In the Bible, God chose a certain man that He wanted to reveal Himself to, a certain man to whom He would entrust a glory story. That man's name was Job.

Job was considered by God to be the most upright and blameless man in all the earth—certainly someone who didn't deserve to have difficulties. But what happened in Job's life wasn't about Job. It was all about God and His desire to prove to Satan that there was at least one person on earth whose love and devotion for God could stand any test. And so the testing began. And, as usually is the case when things go wrong in life, Job had no idea what was going on.

Up to that point in his life, Job had been blessed by God with a family, land, wealth, riches, prestige. He had it all. But in one day—in a matter of hours—God allowed Satan to take it all away. Then God let Satan afflict Job with physical pain and sores all over his body. Job was miserable! And all that time, he didn't know what he had done to deserve this. Job's friends tried to advise him and explain that he was suffering because he had some sin lurking in the corners of his life. Eager to blame Job, they were of no help. Job's wife wasn't any help, either.

Eventually Job cried out to God and asked the question we all ask when we are inundated by troubles: *Why?* But God was silent. Then, toward the end of the story, God broke the silence and spoke. But when He did, He didn't answer Job's questions. Instead, He reminded Job—in a reminder that runs four chapters—that He was the Creator and Sustainer of life and He knew what He was doing. In other words, God was telling Job, "I am God and you are not!"

Job was humbled into silence. He had come face-to-face with

the living God, and the answers to his questions didn't seem to matter anymore. And when Job finally spoke again, he acknowledged God's greatness. Then Job said something profound, something that summed up the work of God in his life: "My ears had heard of you but now my eyes have *seen* you" (Job 42:5, emphasis added).

Job had gone through hell and back in his trials, and in the process he saw God, learned of His ways, understood the depths of His character, and had a greater sense of awe for His power and might.

That, to me, is amazing! God is so powerful and so deserving of glory that He used Job to show His power and might to Satan. Yet at the same time, He is so loving that He wanted to show Job another side of Himself so that Job wouldn't be one of those people who had just heard about God; he could be a person who had *experienced* Him.

God still works the same way today with you and me. He is God and He is deserving of glory, so He can use any one of us to prove His power and might to anyone. Yet He is so loving and so desiring of a relationship with us that He wants to show us another side of Himself so that we, too, won't be women who just "believe in God" or "have heard of God" but women who have *experienced* Him.

Olivia's Ordeal

Olivia came to experience God when she was walking alone in her trials. And today, she says what Job once said: "I had heard of God, believed in Him, and prayed to Him. But now I truly know Him because of the way I have met Him face-to-face." Olivia has a glory story. But when her trial of all trials first started, she never imagined that God could've used any of it to make her stronger and to enlarge her view of Him.

Nearly 20 years ago, Olivia had left her home, family, and everything she knew, including a longtime career, to follow her husband to the West Coast, where he got a job. They were going to start a new life together in California. But within a week after relocating, Olivia discovered her husband had been seeing another woman.

"Suddenly, along with dealing with the stress of making a major cross-country move, I found myself with no friends or family, no church, no belongings [everything would remain in storage for three months until their new house was built], no job for the first time in 20 years, and no husband! With everything removed from me, I lost it emotionally, physically, and even spiritually. I got to the point where I didn't believe even God could love me because I felt so rejected. I never in my life had questioned God's love for me. But that started my journey alone, where God would get my attention and help me understand how much He loved me and wanted to be my source of strength."

For the next eight years, Olivia stood for reconciliation in her marriage, trusting that if God wanted her to remain married, she would and would work through the pain of her husband's betrayal. "I really wanted it to work if there was a chance," she said. But the betrayal worsened through the years as her husband secretly kept his illicit relationship and eventually impregnated his girlfriend. (That was especially difficult for Olivia, who had spent years going through fertility treatments and surgeries in an attempt to get pregnant.) Shortly after Olivia discovered the other woman's pregnancy, Olivia's husband moved out and served her with divorce papers.

Olivia remembers the day a visitor came to her door with the divorce papers. "The reality of being served suddenly hit me and I freaked out," she said. She sat on the floor of her walk-in closet, unable to move, paralyzed by fear. She called a friend, who talked with her about Jesus' sufferings and then prayed with her over the phone for a couple of hours. When Olivia got off the phone, she realized that if Jesus could go to the cross for her sins, she could go to the door and accept the consequences of her husband's sins. "The only way I was able to go out the door that day was knowing that the Lord went before me. If I was served the divorce papers, the Lord was served them first, and would help me and strengthen me."

The Lord became Olivia's strength during that difficult time and the agonizing years that followed. And He began weaving a glory story into her life while she was still in the midst of the pain.

"Throughout my entire trial, the Lord allowed people to cross my path who had already been there so they could encourage me, or were several steps and sometimes years behind me so I could encourage them. Because I was so greatly helped by people, I am committed to helping and encouraging others in their struggles no matter what they are facing."

Today, Olivia looks at the path that her ex-husband chose—the path of disobedience and bitterness—and she rejoices that God didn't allow her to take the same path.

"I can live with myself knowing I did all I could to salvage the marriage, and he was the one who was disobedient. And I have the peace that comes from knowing God was with me every step of the way."

Olivia shudders to think of where her life would be today had she run from God in her trial. Instead, she is happy, healthy, and serving God in her local church.

"I'm stronger today because of the path of suffering I had to walk alone," she said. And others know it. Olivia leads the singles ministry at her church and is a pillar of strength to young women who now walk alone. Through Olivia's trials and troubles, her life and her losses, God has another glory story.

Just as Erin's story reminds me of Job and how he went through his struggles and got to know a side of God that he hadn't experienced before, Olivia's story reminds me of a woman in the Bible named Naomi. Poor Naomi…she once thought her life was over, but she had no idea God was working in and through and around her to accomplish something even greater in someone *else's* life. Look with me at this story of a woman who was bitter at life's circumstances, but soon saw that they were, in time, blessings.

Naomi's Nightmare

Naomi lost all the men in her life—her husband and her two sons—and was left in a foreign land feeling very much alone. Life couldn't get much worse for Naomi. Her response to all this was apparent as she headed back to her hometown and told all her old friends, "Don't call me Naomi anymore; call me Mara," which meant "bitterness." How sad! This miserable woman felt the only word that could sum up her very existence was the word *bitter.*

But God had a purpose for Naomi's life...and it was far bigger than her own sense of comfort and happiness with her husband and two married sons around. God apparently allowed Naomi to lose her husband and sons so she could invest her life in someone else—her widowed daughter-in-law, Ruth. Ruth was a Moabite woman, possibly one who didn't believe in the true God of Israel. And when Naomi's husband and sons died and she set out to leave Moab and return to Israel, her daughter-in-law Ruth decided to go with her. After they arrived in Israel, Ruth married a man related to Naomi and had a baby, and that baby brought great joy to Naomi! What's more, he was an ancestor of the future King David, and years later, Jesus the Messiah. Yes, God had a bigger plan—a plan for a lineage that would bear the Messiah, who would come to save the world.

When Naomi was counting her losses, she felt alone and bitter. But toward the end of her life, when she held her grandson in her arms, she realized God had had a plan all along, and her life turned out to be a blessing after all. I'm convinced that Naomi's divine appointment in life was to teach Ruth to be a godly woman, a good wife, and a good mother. Naomi, who once defined her life as bitter, had a glory story after all.[1]

Your Glory Story

Is your life looking bitter these days? Are you finding yourself inundated by trials or counting your losses? Perhaps God is writing a glory story in your life for someone else's benefit. Naomi's trials led her to help Ruth. Olivia's trials led her to help countless single women. And I believe Erin's trials will lead her to a place where she is a blessing to others as well. Could it be that God has plans for another woman who will benefit from the experiences and lessons you have learned in your personal trials? Is there someone whom you can pour your life into as you go through your difficulties so God can get a glory story?

It's natural for us to say, "No way. My life's a mess. I can't possibly encourage anyone else because of where I am right now." But I have found that it is the pain in my life that I've gone through and the troubles and trials that make me most effective in ministering to women. When I stand and share with women about God's ability to be my Husband, my listeners don't connect until I share about the deserts I've walked through in my own marriage. When I talk of God's love and acceptance, women don't relate until I share where I've gone to find that love and acceptance outside of His arms. When I speak of God's joy in my soul, I am not credible until I share the depths from which God has pulled me and the fact that I can still smile because of who He is. When I speak of trusting Him fully, it sounds like I'm giving a formula until I share the ways I've had to trust Him fully during the shakeups and storms in my own life. The more experience you have in suffering and the more times you walk alone in your trials, the more access you will have to other women's hearts and the wider the doors will swing open for you to help and encourage women in your church, job, or neighborhood who are suffering, too.

Asking the Questions

Usually we question God when we're in a heap of trouble—when a husband walks out, or we're diagnosed with a debilitating or life-threatening disease, when we miscarry a baby or can't get pregnant, or we never get married or lose someone we love. And yet God knows what He is doing. We might not *ever* know why He allows certain things to happen in our lives, but we can be assured that He knows what He's doing and He has promised it will be for our good.

I often hear people say, "That's one of the questions I'll ask Him when I get to heaven." But I believe when we get to heaven we will be so preoccupied with praising God for His grace and love and the sacrifice of His Son that our questions about our sufferings here on earth will be the furthest thing from our minds. Perhaps we'll see the scars in Jesus' hands and see the nail holes in His feet, and they'll remind us that what we went through here on earth was *nothing* compared to what He went through to get us into heaven. Maybe we'll finally understand the apostle Paul's words in Romans 8:18: "I consider that the sufferings of this present time are not worthy to be compared with the glory that is to be revealed to us" (NASB).

We might even be wishing we could face *more* trying circumstances so that we can experience a little more of His glory while we're still here on earth.

Strength in Our Suffering

I have learned in my own life that God uses pain and suffering to mold me in ways that nothing else could. Can I share with you some of the things I've learned so that they can be a source of encouragement to you as you walk alone in your trials?

Trials Transform Our Character

In James 1:2-3, we are told to "consider it all joy...when you encounter various trials, knowing that the testing of your faith produces endurance, and let endurance have its perfect result, so that you may be perfect and complete, lacking in nothing" (NASB). Consider our trials all joy? That hardly seems possible. But when we focus on the outcome—the women we are becoming through the process, the glory story that is being written on the fabric of our lives, the ministry God is developing for us and through us that will one day encourage many others—it can give us reason to smile again.

A woman named Carole sent me a letter about the trials she had walked through over the past 20 years. Her husband walked out on her after 20 years of marriage, she had one child who was taking illegal drugs, her 25-year-old son was killed after a fall from a roof, and she had estranged relationships with her daughters. Yet in all of this, she pursued her relationship with God and trusted that He had a purpose and a plan.

"The glory of it is that I am now 64 and I continue to grow stronger in my walk with the Lord," she wrote. She signed her letter: "In His Refining Fire." That's where Carole has been for the past 20 years—and in the midst of it all, she continues to grow stronger. Carole can consider her trials pure joy, knowing that the testing of her faith has produced endurance, and that endurance has led her to be made more perfect and complete, and stronger in Him.

Trials Shape Us for Eternity

When God promises in His Word that He causes all things to work together for good to those that love Him (Romans 8:28), He follows that promise with the reasons why. It's not so that we can be happy people and feel like we have lived a good and productive life. God's reasons go far deeper than that. He tells us in the following verse that He works all things—even the bad things—together for good because He has an eternal plan for us. "For those God foreknew he also predestined *to be conformed to the likeness of His Son*" (verse 29, emphasis added). There it is! Our trials are designed to make us more like Jesus.

God promises that when we go through difficult circumstances He will see to it that those situations help mold us into the person He wants us to be…and that is a person like His Son—holy, blameless, effective for Him. So if God wants to mold us into women who are utterly dependent on Him, He may allow certain things to happen in our lives that uproot our strongholds and cause us to look to Him for security and dependence—not money, position, status, family, or relationships.

Trials Teach Us of Jesus

Jesus is described in Scripture as a man of sorrows (Isaiah 53:3). He gave up many things, including His life, for you and me. Perhaps finding ourselves alone or rejected or betrayed or misunderstood is one way that we can relate to what He endured here on earth. It might seem like a big price to pay, but in exchange, we get to know personally and more fully the Almighty God.

The apostle Paul, who wrote much of the New Testament, endured more than a fair share of trials: He was imprisoned (several times), severely flogged, beaten with rods (three times), whipped with 39 lashes (five times), shipwrecked (three times), spent a day and a half in the open sea, nearly stoned to death (only once!), and was constantly being robbed, left for dead, and pursued by people who wanted to kill him.[2] Yet this man said all of that was *nothing* compared to the glory and rewards of knowing God and spending an eternity with Him. Wow! How could Paul say that? How could he say all he had endured was *nothing*? He could say it because he had his eyes fixed on the glory story that God was writing and the day he would kneel before his Savior in heaven and say, "It was worth it because it gave me just a glimpse of what You endured for me, my precious Lord."

Could you and I take our trials and suffering (which most likely pale in comparison to Paul's list!) and say, like Paul, that they were *nothing*? I think once we focus on God's purpose for us, we can.

Trials Help Us Comfort and Minister to Others

The Bible tells us that God comforts us in all our trials so that we not only see and experience His comfort in our lives, but also pass that comfort on to others as well (2 Corinthians 1:3-4). What a privilege that He would work in our lives directly, ministering to us through our trials, so that we can then minister to someone else by sharing what God has shown us or giving the comfort He has given us. Will you receive His comfort now so you can pass it on to someone else? God gets a glory story when you do. And if you ever wonder why there are women coming into your life who have experienced the same trials you've endured, wonder no longer. God is bringing them to you so they can learn what you have learned from God!

It's All About Him

Did you notice in the aforementioned points the words *transform, eternity, Himself, others*? It's not really about us, is it? It's all about God and *His* idea of what we should become, *His* eternal plan, *His* revelation of Himself, *His* desire that we encourage others. It's all about *Him*. Perhaps John the Baptist knew that well when he said of Jesus,

"He must become greater; I must become less" (John 3:30). That should be our attitude when we walk alone in our trials. We need to let Jesus become bigger than us and our troubles. We need to recognize He is the One we must lean on to get through. We need to let Him loom larger and larger in our lives until He is all that we can see. And what a glorious view it is!

What About You?

Are you starting to gain some confidence, some sort of feeling that all that you are going through is not for nothing? I hope so. My motto for women who walk alone in their trials is "Don't let it be for nothing." Recycle it, let God redeem it, and use it and turn it into a glory story. In some aspects, it's the only way we can keep our sanity because many times we won't understand the trials we face. It helps a little when we can see that they made us stronger and they gave God glory. But it's up to us whether or not God will get the glory. We can make our desert of trials into a pity party, or turn it into a glory story. It's our choice.

Can I share with you the things that have helped steer my sufferings into the direction of a glory story?

1. *Realize that God is God.* God's answers to Job hold true to us today. He is the Creator and Sustainer. He has sole rights to all He makes. He is in control, whether we admit it or not. He is God and we are not. When we realize this, it puts us and our lives in perspective.

2. *Respect His right to do as He will.* In Galatians 2:20, the apostle Paul, who was determined to give his life over for God's glory story, said, "I have been crucified with Christ and I no longer live, but Christ lives in me." Do you believe that? Do you consider your body His and not your own? When we come to that place of denying ourselves any rights and giving God full control, He blesses us in extraordinary ways. He doesn't always eliminate the trials, but He blesses, nonetheless, by giving us a greater ability to see Him and understand His ways and live in His joy. And when we surrender ourselves to Him, we are in good hands. He is the potter; we are the clay. Just as a parent knows how to steer a child in the right direction,

God knows what He's doing with you. Will you trust Him with your life…all of it?

3. *Recite often what He's done in your life.* By getting into the practice of telling others about God's ongoing goodness in spite of the grievances you've faced, you're revising and updating your glory story. It becomes your testimony. And because God's blessings and care never end, we will always have new things to tell. If you're still telling a glory story of what God did in your life 20 years ago, that's fine, but that shouldn't be the only one you have. We should be able to find more recent examples of His goodness as well—and share them.

My friend Ginny is an example of someone who constantly has a glory story. (Notice I didn't say someone who's constantly going through trials.) Ginny has experienced an abusive first marriage, a divorce, a son on drugs (in jail and now involved in the occult), and the unending trials of trying to adopt her granddaughter. Yet Ginny says, "I believe God has allowed all this garbage-y stuff in my life so I can see Him and depend on Him and be a testimony to others of what He's done in me."

Ginny has that opportunity every time someone complains to her about how bad their life is. She shares a summary of her trials and then recounts the goodness and faithfulness of the God who is in control of all that happens in her life. After hearing Ginny, most women say, "If Ginny can trust God in all that *she's* gone through, then I can trust Him, too."

4. *Rest in the fact that He goes before you.* There's nothing like knowing God is there and He's gone before you! As you walk through your trials, remember that you are not alone. The God who led you there or allowed you to get there walks before you. And His promise to you is this:

> When you pass through the waters, I will be with you; and when you pass through the rivers, they will not sweep over you. When you walk through the fire, you will not be burned; the flames will not set you ablaze (Isaiah 43:2).

5. *Rejoice, for this time will pass.* In Psalm 30, David sings, "Weeping may remain for a night, but rejoicing comes in the morning" (verse 5). That is a promise that the desert of suffering is not forever. It sometimes lasts as long as the night—as long as it takes for you to cling to Him in the night and for Him to get His glory—and then morning will come. David ends his song with these encouraging words: "You turned my wailing into dancing; you removed my sackcloth and clothed me with joy, *that my heart may sing to you* and not be silent. O Lord my God, I will give you thanks forever" (verses 11-12, emphasis added). With as many trials as David had been through, he knew each one would eventually come to an end. And that is where he tried to keep his focus.

The exhortation to rejoice no matter what our circumstances is given by Paul in Philippians 4:4: "Rejoice in the Lord always. I will say it again: Rejoice!" Paul wrote those words from prison, knowing that his suffering wasn't forever. Perhaps just knowing that your suffering is only for a season will help you rejoice, too—even when you don't feel like it.

Get Ready to Sing

Perhaps the single most important fact for you to remember, my friend, is that your trials are not forever. If you remain faithful, they will accomplish what God has intended. As promised in Psalm 30, He will turn *your* crying into dancing as well. He will remove *your* dark clothes and cover you in joy, too.

And when He does—and perhaps before He does!—I hope your heart, too, will sing…of His goodness and His provision and His blessing, in spite of your circumstances. And I hope that, like the psalmist, you will not be silent, but that you will instead tell the world your glory story!

Finding Your Glory Story

For Personal Application

1. Read 2 Corinthians 1:3-4. Write down some of the ways in which you have experienced God's comfort in your trials or present circumstances. As you look over what you have written, think of someone who would be encouraged by what you have received from God. Then make a point of connecting with that person, through a phone call, email, letter, or a lunch date, and share with her your glory story.

2. The Bible says to be thankful in all things. Another way we could say this is to see the glass as half full instead of half empty. Make a mental (or written) list of the difficult circumstances you are wading through, and then thank God for each of them. He will smile on your act of obedience to be thankful in *all* things.

3. Look up the following verses. Personalize them and summarize them in terms of God writing your glory story:

    Psalm 13:

    Psalm 30:4-5:

Psalm 31:7-8:

Romans 8:28-29:

James 1:2-3:

4. Pick one of the five steps on pages 128-130 and concentrate on it this week. In subsequent weeks, pick another step, and another. You will be amazed at how your perspective in each of these areas will begin shaping you along the lines of your unique glory story.

For Further Study

In your Bible, read the book of Job. I know it's long, but it's a fascinating story—one you'll be blessed to read in its entirety. (If you can't manage all 42 chapters, at least read Job 1–3:1, then consider how Job's friends try to determine the cause of his condition and note Job's response. Then read God's amazing response to Job in chapters 38–41, and then the conclusion of the story in chapter 42.)

According to Job 1–3:1, what is Satan's reason for messing with Job?

How does God express confidence in Job?

What two conditions does God lay out to Satan in order to protect Job? (Hint: Job 1:12 and 2:6.)

What is Job's initial reaction to his suffering (see Job 1:20-22)?

Whom or what does Job end up cursing as a result of his suffering (see 3:1)?

How does Job respond after his friends attempt to diagnose his condition (3:1-13)?

What is Job's attitude toward God all through this tremendous amount of suffering (13:15)?

What impresses you the most about God's response in Job 38–41? (Many of the lines are poetic—list a few of your favorites, including truths that you find mind-boggling.)

What does Job then express in 42:1-2?

List Job's physical and material awards for his obedience and trust in God (at least ten are described in 42:10-17).

What was Job's spiritual and eternal reward for his suffering (42:5)?

As you reflect on Job's account, thank God that you have never experienced the extent of suffering that he did. Thank and praise God that his servant, Job, passed this test, and thank Him for the tests He gives to you.

PART THREE

A Season of Soaring

"Those who hope in the Lord will renew their strength. They will soar on wings like eagles…"

—Isaiah 40:31

Alone in Your Restlessness:
BECOMING DESPERATE FOR GOD

I'm in a place in life where I don't want to be right now," Valerie said with desperation in her voice. She had just arrived at the same age her mother was when she began a "mid-life crisis" that eventually led to an affair.

"I just feel so restless…like I'm out of control and I actually could do the same thing. I don't have a reason, though. Jeff has been wonderful. So I have absolutely no reason to be feeling the way I do. But I still feel this way.

"All my life I've been the responsible one. I had to have it all together as the oldest of three kids. I never got a chance to rebel. I just feel like I want to live a little, do my rebelling, experience what I never got to before."

"What exactly are you saying, Val?" I asked her.

"I don't know…I just feel a restlessness within me to do something really stupid!"

Valerie and I talked about her ministry position at her church. We discussed the fact that she didn't have an option to rebel because of the cost of that rebellion to her husband, her children, her friends, and the people she ministered to. We talked about the lie of having to sin in order to "live a little" and how the only life worth living is a life that is obedient to Jesus. We talked of how "sin for a season" leads to death.[1]

Valerie knew all that. But still, she felt restless.

Call it a mid-life crisis, or a selfish phase, or sin. Valerie was entering a season of her life in which she desperately wanted *something*.

What was at the root of her restlessness?

Although Valerie knew God and served Him faithfully at her church, she wasn't *desperate* for Him. She wasn't able to say, like David in Psalm 42:1, "My soul pants for you, O God." And so, when the winds of restlessness began to blow—because of an aging body, or a lack of fulfilled dreams, or a series of disappointments, or a mild state of depression—she began panting for something, *anything* to fill the void she was feeling. Because she wasn't desperate for God, her heart in a season of restlessness became desperate for something else. And that desperation was waiting to destroy her.

Desperately Seeking Something

Restlessness—which can often turn into desperation—is nothing new to women. We've been desperately seeking something since the beginning of time. Eve was restless in the Garden of Eden—the most beautiful, perfect place on earth—because there was something she wanted *more* than God. She wanted the knowledge of good *and* evil. Because of that desperation she disobeyed God, and it resulted in her eventual death.[2]

Sarah, Abraham's wife, was restless about not having a child. And she became desperate when God's promise to give her a son didn't come as soon as she had hoped. Thirteen years into the 25-year wait that God had intended, she gave her maid to her husband and got a son through her maid...but her desperate action produced grave consequences.[3]

Rachel, the wife that Jacob loved more than Leah (remember them in chapter 2?) was so desperate for children that when she finally had a child, she was already talking about having another one![4] Then, when she gave birth to her second son, she named him "son of my sorrow" and then died. Ironically, the one thing she wanted most in life ended up taking her life. Her desperation for something other than God literally killed her!

I could go on and on with the stories, but I think the point is clear. We were designed with the capacity to love God with all our heart, mind, soul, and strength. But if we direct our heart, mind, soul, and strength toward something or someone other than God, it could destroy us.

God once told a restless man, "Sin is crouching at your door; it desires to have you, but you must master it" (Genesis 4:7). God knows we are people of passion. But He wants that passion directed toward Himself so we don't mess up our lives…and the lives of others.

Directing Our Desperation

My friend Edie weathered quite a few restless seasons in life without resorting to some desperate means, particularly because she was determined to see how God was shaping her heart and mind to follow Him. Edie stands out to me as a woman who sought God in the midst of her restless times and because of that, grew stronger through them.

Edie grew up with a mentally ill father, a mother who wouldn't deal with the situation, and three older brothers, so she never felt like she fit in—anywhere. She went through a season of restlessness as a child, as a young wife who expected her husband to make up emotionally for what she didn't get from her parents, as a woman twice diagnosed with cancer—feeling that God and everyone else had forgotten her—and as an adult daughter caring for her aged mother with dementia. Today, in the aftermath of burying her mother, and her adult sons having left home, Edie looks at life realistically, knowing that another season of aloneness will come, and she will be prepared when it does.

Edie sees loneliness as a part of life, and she looks at the seasons of aloneness in her life as the pieces of one big puzzle designed to make her long for God.

"I believe God allows us to walk through the deserts so we can realize how desperate we are for Him," she said. "All women are desperate for something...shouldn't it be a desperation for God?"

Edie has seen how her loneliness in her marriage has drawn her closer to her heavenly Husband. She's seen how her struggle with cancer (now *three* times!) has deepened her trust in the character of God. She experienced God's sustaining grace daily while she took care of her mother and dealt with the cruel effects of dementia. And she has seen other women encouraged by her own glory stories of how God has worked in and through her life. But even though Edie has weathered many of the seasons that may still be in store for you and me, she by no means thinks it will be smooth sailing from here on out.

"Now I'm looking at getting older, at not having as much energy as I had when I was younger, at not being as quick and sharp as the younger women who are beginning to do the things I used to do. Aging, I guess, is the next season of life that will hit me. But as long as I keep my focus on what's most important, I'll be able to walk through it. I'm already preparing for it by continually asking myself, 'What am I desperate for?'"

Facing the Question

That's a good question for any of us, don't you think? What am I desperate for?

Most women today are desperate for *something*. The headlines on the most popular women's magazines would imply to us that women today are desperate to be thin, attractive, loved, and less stressed.

Women I speak to across the country are desperate to be in a love relationship—if not with a man, then with God—that will satisfy them and fulfill them.

And Valerie, whom we met at the beginning of this chapter, appears to be desperate for youth, excitement, and to feel as if she's "lived."

I remember when I was desperate to find a husband, desperate to have a second child, desperate to feel happy and secure, desperate to fulfill my dreams. What if, in each of those seasons of life, I had asked myself, "Cindi, what are you *really* desperate for right now?" And what if I had followed up that question with, "Cindi, what is the *one thing* you *should* be desperate for right now?"

Perhaps then I would have turned my desire toward the only One who satisfies and I would have endured those seasons like Edie, with an eye toward growing and learning and becoming stronger in the way God had designed me to go.

Focusing on the One Thing

In Psalm 27:4, David says there is *one thing* he desires— one thing he is desperate for—and that is to "dwell in the house of the LORD all the days of my life, to gaze upon the beauty of the LORD and to seek him in his temple." David wanted to live close to God's heart—to know Him and love Him and see His face. David was truly desperate for God. And in his psalms, it is obvious that he will stop at nothing to know God in the way he was designed to.

Now, David had many restless times in his life. But as long as his focus was on his desperation for God, he persevered through those times and became stronger through them. But the times that he lost his focus and became desperate for other things—like another man's wife, or security in the number of fighting men he had—he acted foolishly and brought about very grave consequences on others.[5]

The same was true about Abraham. When he lost his focus on God and disobeyed, there were drastic consequences for a lot of people. And the same thing happens today when women get restless and disobey God. A lot of people end up getting hurt as a result.

My friend Pam often counsels women during their "mid-life crises" or restless times in life. When Pam counsels women, she first listens to their problems (most commonly related to their husband's failures). Pam then explains that "at this pivotal moment she can look to God to meet her needs and her life will be richer and stronger for it, or she can turn away from God and look to other options to meet the needs. When she looks to other options, sin looks justified and the illogical suddenly becomes logical to her."

It's at this point that Pam actually talks out the options so they can really sink in to the woman who is contemplating drastic measures in her desperation.

Pam says, "I ask them, 'Which life would you prefer?' Option one: Take your loneliness to God, let Him meet the need, let Him bless your life and the lives of your children because of your obedience; or, option two: have an affair, and make your kids go through the ravages of a divorce and the disillusionment of having a mom who is a hypocrite. They may lose their home if you have to move, and if so, they will lose their friends and church and community support. This betrayal may lead them to lose faith in all adults, all authority figures, and maybe even lose faith in God, so that they, too, make poor choices and look to sex, drugs, or other unhealthy lifestyles to try to get the vacuum of their soul filled. And once you have *your* needs met, most likely the relationship won't last because the affair wasn't God's will, and then you have that alone feeling back. You may also be a wreck financially by then and have a juvenile delinquent on your hands."

Though it sounds rather extreme, many counselors—including Pam—have seen this scenario play out over and over again. And many times, at the root of it all is a woman who is desperate for *something* other than God.

"When you lay the two options next to each other, the right answer seems obvious: go to God with your restlessness," Pam says.

Now, I realize you most likely would never think of such drastic measures (such as having an affair or doing something "stupid") during a season of restlessness. But because it is so common for women, myself included, to be bombarded with such thoughts that other people, the media, and even the darkness of our own soul throw our way, I wanted to address that. Sometimes just a lingering thought, if unchecked, can turn into a longing...deep in the recesses of our hearts.

Interpreting the Longing

The great poet Goethe once said, "All human longing is really longing for God." That makes sense. When we're young and hoping for true love and a man to marry, if we just longed for God more than a lover, we would endure that season and grow stronger.

As we're trying to have children and perhaps struggling with infertility, we could grow stronger through it, spiritually, if we just realized that God's design for us is to learn that sometimes we can't have exactly what we want right when we want it.

When we experience a season of illness or caring for an ill or aged parent, our restlessness for something different can be directed toward a desire to learn what God wants to teach us about His grace, which can sustain us through whatever He allows to come our way.

And as we struggle in the afternoon of life with an empty nest, a body that doesn't look or work the way it used to, and the feelings of restlessness during retirement, we can adopt the perspective that we can be grateful that God has allowed us to live this long.

Hilda sees retirement as a very different, slower-paced life. But rather than complain because it's different, she is seeing it as her reward from her heavenly Father for her faithful years of working and raising her children in the knowledge of the Lord. She intends to enjoy this season in life as a time to invest in the lives of her grandchildren, rest in the Lord, and grow in her devotion toward God. I pray I can have that perspective as well when I reach that season in life!

I mentioned that at one time I was desperate for a man in my life, but what I really wanted was to be loved…and later, I learned that fulfillment could come only through an intimate relationship with God. I mentioned, too, that I was desperate for a second child, but what I really wanted was to go to that "next step" of where I believed I needed to be in life (after all, not many parents decide to have just one child). And that next step, rather than having another child, was a greater dependence on God. I have recently been desperate for some quiet time in my life—some time to walk away from my many responsibilities and just be by myself (for an extrovert like me, that's pretty unusual!). But what I'm really desperate for is a deeper relationship with God that comes only from stillness and uninterrupted time at His feet.

Karen endured five years of feeling restless and desperate. She had three children in three years, experienced several health problems, watched her children struggle with health problems, went through the transition of her husband's new job pastoring a church, endured the stress of mounting financial pressures, and dealt with continual verbal attacks from one of the women's leaders in her church. She now looks back on that one miserable season of her life with great relief that it's over with. Yet she also recognizes that she grew and matured as a result.

"Just simply aging and having more up-and-down cycles under my belt has helped," she says. "I know that if it seems the Lord is not speaking or moving, it's just a cycle, and when He's ready, He'll be there. I try to ride out the down cycles, trusting that they're temporary, trying to learn what I can, and remembering not to be hard on myself because I've messed up. When God is quiet, it might be because He's not yet ready to speak to me. I guess my advice for other women in similar times would be to hang on and trust God. He is there for you!"

My friend Barbara, who has faced difficult alone times and longings in her life, says, "Our aloneness and restlessness is like a flashing red light designed to get our attention, and when we see our situation as special (as a time when God is drawing us to Himself), then joy and peace will come from our just waiting and being available to the Lord. Cherish the time and know God is waiting to share and partner with you. There will be an added richness in your life that will fill that void called aloneness."

Waiting on God

Christi Kari remembers when that "red light" appeared in her life. Five years into her marriage, she became a Christian and was excited about her new relationship with God. But she was also very restless about the fact that she had not been able to have a child during those five years. After another three years went by, with fertility tests and treatment, she became disillusioned that the Lover of her soul, whom she had met three years earlier, wasn't giving her the desire of her heart (a new baby). She began to think that perhaps if she knew God better, she could figure out why He hadn't given her a child. So she started attending a small Bible study at her church, and that's when she realized that her desperation was on having a child, not on God, where it should be.

"I was obsessed 24 hours a day with what I didn't have," she said. "I had taken my eyes off of God and placed them on myself in my desperation to be a mother."

When a close friend confronted Christi about her heart going after something other than God, Christi repented and began longing for God alone. But still, the baby didn't come. Two years later, Christi's husband finally agreed to adopt a child, and Christi felt she would finally be given her reward for waiting so long on God during her time of desperation. A year later, after being "selected" by a birth mother and after their adopted baby was born, they were called to the hospital to meet and receive their gift from God. But on the way to the hospital, with all their hopes and "baby stuff" in tow, they received a call on their cell phone that the birth mother had changed her mind and decided to keep the baby. Christi and her husband returned home childless—and nearly devastated.

Christi had to hold on to the fact that her heavenly Father was sovereign, loving, and good, and that He knew what He was doing. She chose not to believe that He was dangling a carrot (or, in this case, a baby) in front of her and then continually pulling it away. She chose not to do something desperate out of her frustration and hurt. Instead, she accepted an offer shortly afterward to share her "infertility testimony" with a group of women at her church. Even though Christi didn't want to talk about the hurt and disappointment, she knew that to do so, in a way that would honor God, would be the right thing to do. So she shared her story, publicly praising God for

His goodness in spite of the disappointment and hurt about still not having a baby. Just a week after that, and totally unexpectedly, God put a baby girl into her arms.

"For nine years I had been asking God for a miracle. He gave it to me, but it was according to His will and His timing, not mine," Christi says. "He had to combat the idols in my life—such as pride, my own plans, depending on myself—to get me to the point that He was my one and only God. Not until then could He entrust me with the desire of my heart."

God wanted to be Christi's ultimate desire; He wanted to be the One for whom she was desperate.

Today Christi is the mother of *two* adopted children and is active in a Bible study/care group that she founded for women who struggle with infertility. Christi's tender encouragement to the brokenhearted and restless women she encounters is to direct their desperation toward God and make Him the sole desire of their heart.[6]

Putting It into Practice

So, how do we make sure that God is the one we're desperate for when those inevitable seasons of restlessness blow into our lives? How do we defend against an unhealthy desperation that can destroy us, and instead, turn it into a healthy desperation toward God? Women who have walked before me into deserts of restlessness I have yet to encounter have shared with me these words of wisdom:

Listen to Your Head, Not Your Heart

One of the lies we learn from songs, movies, and modern culture is to "listen to your heart." This theme is depicted in movies where women scrap all that they have to run off with the man they want, because therein will lie "true happiness." In sad-ending movies like *The Bridges of Madison County*, and *Castaway*, the women who decide against the affair and end up staying with their husbands and children are often pitied for doing "the right thing" (and we get the idea that they end up "paying for it" the rest of their lives by their mundane existence, void of the excitement they could've had). Who wants to live that way? No wonder we like the phrase "listen to your heart."

The only problem with listening to our hearts is that, as Jeremiah 17:9 says, "The heart is deceitful above all things and beyond cure. Who can understand it?" Our hearts usually want what *we* want rather than what *God* wants.

Fortunately, my friend Valerie eventually listened to her head, not her heart, and determined that the voices she was hearing were lies from the world and her own deceitful heart, and had nothing to do with "whatever is true, whatever is noble, whatever is right, whatever is pure, whatever is lovely, [and] whatever is admirable" (Philippians 4:8). Praise God for the truth of His Word and His convicting Holy Spirit, which can pierce our hearts and minds! Valerie listened to God's Word and Spirit, and I believe her husband, children, friends, family, church, and Jesus will someday thank her!

We can trust listening to our head, and not our hearts, when we have the truth of God's Word running through our minds to balance the temporal feelings that fluctuate about in our hearts.

Look for the Right Women to Surround You

A friend of mine who is also an author and national speaker has built certain hedges of protection into her life so that she won't "go off the deep end" during certain seasons of life.

"I look for women who are strong in areas that I am weak," she says. "By surrounding myself with quality women, I place a hedge of protection around my life. For example, I am prone to reacting emotionally initially to the feeling of being abandoned, so I purposefully chose to surround myself with women who have faced *real* abandonment issues and looked to God for their strength. For example, in my circle of friends, I have one friend who was abandoned by her birth mom at age seven, was abandoned by her stepmom during elementary school, and had a dad who died of a drug overdose when she was 16. She was on her own financially at 16! I also am friends with several widows, several women who have lost children, and several friends whose husbands left them for other women or were victims of domestic violence. Those women really know what it means to walk alone. I want them in my life because they provide perspective. I know I can share my problems with them, and that they will know how to point me back to God because they have already been on that path. The additional benefit of having women who have really walked alone in certain seasons of life and looked to God for their strength is that I am less prone to feel sorry for myself. When I compare my emotional pain to the real crises they have faced, my life looks a little easier and answers seem to be a little closer."

Are there women you can surround yourself with—women who can bring your alone times into perspective and can keep you on solid ground when you feel like flying the coop?

I myself have already begun to think about the women I want around me for the upcoming seasons in life. I am grateful to have Edie as my friend, for if I'm ever diagnosed with cancer, she's been there, and I know she'll be there for me. If I ever have to care for an aging parent, or when I lose a parent, she's been there, too, so she will know what to say to help me through.

I also have women in my life who have lost a daughter…and if I should ever have to walk through that desert, I know they will understand what I'm going through and will drop what they're doing to be by my side.

The Bible tells us that "two are better than one" because "if one falls down" (or enters a season of restlessness in which she is tempted to go astray), her friend can help her up (Ecclesiastes 4:9-10). "But pity the [one] who falls and has no one to pick [her] up!" (verse 10). We're also told "though one may be overpowered [by temptations or an unhealthy desperation], two can defend themselves. A cord of three strands is not quickly broken" (verse 12). Get some extra strands in your cord by gathering some spiritually healthy women around you as you prepare to meet the impending seasons of life.

Long for God Now, Before the Winds of Restlessness Begin to Blow

Psalm 84:11 tells us the Lord God is a sun and shield. He is a sun because He directs and illumines our way, and He is a shield because He protects us. But He is our sun and shield only so long as we're obedient to Him. If we choose to rebel, then we are spurning His light and His protection. Do you want to be without His guidance and protection? That's what you risk when you let restlessness lure you away from Him. When you truly long for Him, you will find Him as your Fortress and Friend.

Pray for a love for God that grows deeper in your heart every day. The Bible says in 1 John 5:14-15 that we can be confident that when we ask something of Him in His name, He hears us, and we will receive what we asked for. To ask for something in His name is to ask for something that Jesus would ask for. To ask, then, for a passion and love for God above anything else is to ask God for something He promises to give us. Won't you start praying today that God will fill your heart with a desire for Him alone? By doing so, you will make yourself immune to the desires and whims of this world. You will be putting on your shield for those winds of restlessness that perhaps lie ahead.

Leave Your Place of Wishful Thinking

It's easy for us to get caught up in wishful thinking and say to ourselves, *If only I had a husband. If only I had a different husband. If only I had what I used to have. If only there was more excitement in my life.* But such thinking is dangerous, for then we begin to pursue something other than God.

In John chapter 5, we read about the time when Jesus walked into a courtyard in Jerusalem where many people with various ailments were lying around a pool. This pool, called Bethesda, was probably fed by a mineral hot spring just outside the city and was believed to have curative powers. The rumor around town was that an angel periodically came down to the pool to stir up the waters, and whoever was the first one to jump in when the waters bubbled would be cured. We don't know if anyone ever got cured, but we do know quite a lot of people waited by the pool in hopes of getting cured.

When Jesus arrived, there was a paralyzed man who had been lying by the pool for 38 years! When Jesus asked him if he wanted to get well, the man didn't answer Jesus' question. Rather, he gave an excuse for why he was still lying by the pool after all these years! The man had no idea that the Great Healer was in his midst and had just offered to make him whole.

Jesus was intent on helping the man, though, and told him to get up off the ground, grab his mat, and get out of there. When the man listened to Jesus, he found that he could stand and walk! (John 5:1-9).

You and I have pools of Bethesda in our lives, as well. We sometimes find ourselves waiting by a pool of expectation, believing that if someone came and stirred things up in our life, we'd be happier. And if we're not careful, we can become like the paralyzed man, stuck on the road of false expectations for years! But Jesus doesn't want us to live that way. He made us for something better! He wants to lead us away from the pool of false expectations and into the reality of an abundant life close to His side.

My friend, do you realize the same Healer who walked by the pool of Bethesda stands waiting to help you get up and walk away from that heap of hopes that has left you disappointed, that pool of dashed dreams that has left you debilitated, that sea of restlessness that has you spellbound? He will help you get up and walk with strength through *any* season of your life. You just have to recognize that He is the *way* to true help; He is the *truth* in the midst of lies; and He is the *life* that ignites our soul with hope (John 14:6). And in case you didn't catch it by now, Jesus is the *only* Spring of Living Water that can make us whole and satisfy our soul.

Get Ready to Run!

Are you ready to not only get through this season of your life but run through it? Then get up, grab your mat of false expectations, and go after the One who holds your life and your plans and your destiny in His hands. There is no other place to be!

Here are some encouraging words from Psalm 62 to guide you as you follow Him away from the pool of restless waters:

> My soul finds rest in God alone; (not those other things I want); my salvation comes from him. He alone is my rock and my salvation; he is my fortress, I will never be shaken (Psalm 62:1-2).

Oh, to be able to say that: I will *never* be shaken—not by desertion, not by divorce, not by desperation for something I can never have. I will never be shaken because of the One who is holding me firm…because of the One on whom I have built my foundation.

In the next few verses, David speaks of the world and its attempts to assault him, throw him down, and topple him. He then instructs himself, "Find rest, O my soul, in God alone; my hope comes from Him…My salvation and my honor depend on God; He is my mighty rock, my refuge" (verses 5-7).

Do you realize, O woman of God, that your honor depends on Him? We can blow it big time if we are not fully grounded in Him during the seasons of restlessness in our lives and the temptations that come along with them.

Look at how David ends his song—it's like he's summing up the best advice he's ever had in life: "One thing God has spoken, two things have I heard: that you, O God, are strong, and that you, O Lord, are loving. Surely you will reward each person according to what he has done" (verses 11-12).

That's good to remember in life. That God is strong, and able to get us through whatever comes our way. And He is loving. He will not allow anything to come our way that is not for our eternal good. Once we become convinced that God is strong and God is loving, we can endure *any* season because we can live in the hope that He will reward us. And perhaps that reward will be a heart that is desperate for God alone.

Developing a Desperation for God

For Personal Application

1. Make a list of the women whom you need to surround yourself with at this stage in life and the seasons to come. Pray that God will bring those women into your life to help hold you up and help you have a right perspective.

2. Take some time to thank God right now for the women He has already brought into your life who are positively influencing you and helping you keep a spiritual perspective. Now go the extra mile by sending cards in the mail or writing emails to some of these women, thanking them for their positive influence in your life. These are among your priority relationships. Let these women know that.

3. Read Psalm 26:2-3 and write it out, in your own words, as a prayer from your heart. Or, write a prayer to God incorporating your season of restlessness into it. Share that prayer with a trusted friend or your study group, if that will help.

4. Think and pray about the one thing you want. Ask God to give you a desperation for Him alone so that He becomes the one thing you want. Write out Psalm 27:4 or Psalm 73:25 and put the verse in a place where it will remind you of the one thing worth pursuing.

For more on this subject, see my book *Women on the Edge: Turning Desperate Times into Desire for God* (Eugene, OR: Harvest House, 2010).

For Further Study

Look at David's situation in Psalm 13.

    a. What is he feeling in verses 1-2?

    b. Where is his focus in verse 3 (to whom is he calling)?

    c. What facts is he able to recite in verses 5-6?

Did you notice what changed David's pity in the first few verses to praise in the last couple of verses? It was *prayer*! How can this psalm be a model for how you can handle a desperate season in your life?

According to Proverbs 4:23, why is it important to guard your heart?

According to Jeremiah 17:9, why should you listen to your head and not your heart?

What does Philippians 4:6 say we should do when we begin to feel anxious or worried? And what does verse 7 say will happen as a result?

What types of things does Philippians 4:8 say we should focus our minds on? (List the characteristics here.)

Alone in Your Dreams:
KNOWING GOD IS FOR YOU

elissa was bursting with excitement. The dream God had placed in her heart to open a home for single mothers was beginning to be realized. She had help, prayer, financial support, and enthusiasm from people everywhere she turned. A woman in her church offered to lease a seven-bedroom house to her and help her with the work. Someone else offered to help budget a savings plan for the ministry. Others offered to help with the paperwork in filing for a nonprofit status. And when the question of funding arose, things came together that enabled Melissa to open a thrift store in one of the rooms of the home to help support the ministry.

But within about two months, the woman who was leasing the home to Melissa became uncommitted to both the home and the thrift store, the person who offered to help with the budgeting also wanted to back out, and the lady who helped with the nonprofit paperwork fell ill. Within what seemed like no time at all, Melissa, who was once surrounded with support and enthusiasm, was left holding onto her dream all alone. Having lost her support system and the people she believed would be there to the end, she began to wonder if she should just give up on this dream altogether.

It was then that she remembered who it was who called her to the task. "I really struggled with the question of whether or not I would be equipped enough to see this dream through," she said. "Finally I decided that I was."

She was equipped not because she was secure financially or had the promises of others to help her out. Rather, she was equipped because the One who placed the dream in her heart would provide what she needed to see it through.

"My mom reminded me that this was my burden, not someone else's, and I can't expect anyone here on earth to understand," Melissa said. "This was a God-given vision, and I needed to depend on God."

Melissa has done that and found that her God has been faithful. She has also found that when God is the One whispering the dream into her ear, He is also the One who ultimately makes it happen.

The last time I talked with Melissa, Hannah's Inn Ministries (H.I.M., which also stands for Helping Infants and Mothers) was still providing a place for single mothers and their babies. There have been months when the rent on the house was just barely paid, but it has been paid nonetheless. God has kept the doors open. He has kept the dream alive.

And He has strengthened Melissa through the journey of walking alone in her dreams.

"When I focus on people I become discouraged, depressed, and ready to give up," she says. But when she focuses on the Lord, she remembers who it is who can do through her what is beyond her.

"The experience I have gained and the knowledge and the spiritual training I have received through all of this has made me a stronger person," she said. "I know now that I do walk alone in my dream, but my spirit is never alone. When no one else understands, that's okay, because I know Someone who does understand. It took me a long time to realize that I don't need a person with a house or a person with a budget. I don't need money and I don't need a support system if it's not there. All I need is God; everything else is in His hands. And I'm so thankful I learned this at age 27, not 57!"

For Melissa, walking alone in her dreams is a part of life, but she realizes she is not really alone. Someone goes before her, working out every last detail, handling the behind-the-scenes arrangements and assuring her—just in time—that she *can* walk in His plan and accomplish the dreams He has placed in her heart.

Pam's Pursuit

Pam Workman had a dream, too. But she didn't need money, people, or a place to help her fulfill her calling. She needed something that people couldn't supply: a healthy dose of confidence that she could rise above her past, her insecurities, and her perceived obstacles in order to be all that God had called her to be. Pam was 37 and had been following Jesus for only three years when she saw the need in her church for a women's ministry—one that would provide opportunities for women in all stages of life to serve God and use their gifts to please Him.

But she was up against a few walls. One was the wall of resistance: starting a new way of doing things in a nearly 100-year-old church wasn't easy. Change was difficult, and often people were resistant. She was also up against the wall of intimidation: Who was *she* to suggest such a change and offer to be the one to bring it about? She was so new in the faith and certainly didn't have the experience for what she was hoping to do. And she was up against the wall of insecurity: From the time she was a child in an emotionally and physically abusive home, to her marriage at age 18 while three months pregnant, and then living the next 15 years pursuing whatever she felt would fill her soul, she always felt alone, inadequate, and completely unqualified to do anything.

But Pam loved God. And He was giving her a love for other women and a desire to serve them. So Pam stepped out of her comfort zone and approached her pastor about starting a women's ministry at her church. She remembers feeling so alone as she proposed the idea.

"It was just me and God. I was starting a new thing in our church and sometimes change doesn't go over very well...especially from someone like me, who had a past and no experience. I hadn't even graduated from high school. I was scared to death.

"I didn't like to speak in front of others and had never led a committee to start anything!" And then she had to deal with the voices in her head that nagged her about her past: *Why are you the one who wants to do this? People know how you used to live. What will convince them that you have changed? No one else is in on this with you. You can't do it alone.*

But Pam realized she was not alone.

"I knew in my heart it was what the Lord wanted me to do. I guess those old tapes were playing in my mind—tapes of rejection and thoughts of *I can't do this.* My past came up quite a bit in my thoughts, and I had only been a believer for three years. *But,* I thought, *if the Lord wants me to do this, He will make a way.*"

And He did.

Pam stepped into a paid position as a women's ministry director at her church, got a team of women to share in her vision, and within a couple years had developed a thriving women's ministry at her church.

But five years later, the pastor who had hired Pam and helped instill a sense of confidence in her left the church—along with the associate pastor, the youth pastor, and three women on Pam's leadership team.

For a while, from Pam's perspective, it seemed her ministry—and the church—was drifting on a sea of uncertainty without direction or leadership. It was then that her insecurities pressured her to walk out, too. *Why are you staying? No one's supporting you anymore; everyone else is walking out. No one really appreciates what you're doing. In a few months there won't be a job left for you anyway.*

But Pam pressed on, knowing that the One who had whispered the dream into her ear would be the One who would see her through.

A new pastor eventually came to fill the pulpit, and her church entered a new era of growth. The women's ministry continued with her at the helm for several more years until she trained up a new leader.

Like Melissa, Pam felt alone in her journey to fulfill the calling she believes God placed on her heart. And like Melissa, Pam looked to God, not others, for her applause and affirmation. She learned a lot about peacemaking and dealing with conflict over the past several years. She learned to work through difficult times and encourage others to do the same. She's learned not to run from problems, even though she has felt like it many times. But mostly, she has learned that when God is for her, no one can be against her (Romans 8:31).

Pursuing the Dream

Pursuing your dream can be a difficult and lonely journey if you don't feel you have anyone behind you. There's a saying that behind every great man is an equally great woman. I think that's because, for years, the women did the encouraging and supporting and behind-the-scenes campaigning to push their husbands into the spotlight. But who pushes women into the arena of their dreams? Their husbands? Other women? I believe in most cases, they pretty much depend on God alone.

A friend of mine remembers having to battle her husband to go to school again to pursue her dreams. For a while, he didn't feel it was necessary. They had three children, he had a successful ministry, and they were happy. But for her, there was a dream waiting to be fulfilled. And her husband eventually realized that God was placing a dream in her heart and a call on her life, and she had to follow!

Several years ago when I pursued my desire to get some of my writing in print, I went through month after month of getting rejection letters from Christian publishers. Nobody seemed sympathetic whenever I got another one of those discouraging letters in my mailbox. I remember the day I tossed my third rejection letter in one month into the trash and mumbled something about just giving up. Then my husband said, "What if you quit before the one time it was destined to happen?"

Destined to happen? His statement reminded me that the God who loves us intimately and is aware of the details of our dreams is in control of all things and brings all things about in His time—not earlier, and not later.

Then I attended a Christian writer's conference and heard a literary agent give a pep talk to us discouraged writers who were about to quit. "Only *you* can kill the dream that God has put into your heart to write," the agent said. I thought long and hard about that. God did plant that dream in my heart—a dream that goes back to my childhood. When I was only six years old, I was writing stories for my friends. God further developed and shaped that dream through high school and my college years, when I majored in journalism and started getting jobs writing for newspapers. God refined that dream as I left the secular newspaper arena and began writing Bible studies for women. To quit when I got discouraged would be to squash what He'd been directing and calling me to do all my life.

Recognizing God's sovereignty in my hopes and dreams—as well as my life—gave me a fresh perspective. I found verse after verse of encouragement in His Word that I applied toward my God-confidence in fulfilling my dream.

Within a couple months of gaining my new perspective, I drafted an entirely new book—one that developed out of what God was teaching me in my life—and began speaking on it. A few months after that, on my second submission attempt, that book was accepted for publication. I remember the day my editor called me and told me the book proposal was going before the publishing committee for consideration.

"It's difficult for unknown writers to get books published these days," he told me. "But God is sovereign over publishing committees." There it was again, that affirmation of God's complete control. God was sovereign…against the odds…and He allowed that book proposal to become a book that has continued to impact women's lives and help them grow in their relationship with God.

Being alone in your dreams can be a frightful thing—until you realize you are not really alone.

Facing the Impossible

It's easy to look at a situation and think of reasons we *can't* be successful. Like Melissa, we might ask ourselves, "Where will I get the money to pursue this?" Or like Pam, we might ask, "Why on earth do I think *I* can do this?" Maybe for you the question is this: "How can I possibly go back to school at this time in my life?" or, "Who am I to start my own business and think I can succeed?" Or maybe you're saying, "How am I going to accomplish this thing God is laying on my heart? It's too big…and I have no experience, no qualifications, no connections." But when we say those things, we're forgetting the One who is our experience, our qualification, and our major Connection.

Jesus' disciples asked those same kinds of questions, even after they had seen Him do miracles and were physically at Jesus' side.

In Mark chapter 8, we find that a large crowd had gathered around Jesus for three days straight to hear Him teach, and they didn't have anything to eat. So Jesus told His disciples, "I have compassion for these people; they have already been with me three days and have nothing to eat. If I send them home hungry, they will collapse on the way, because some of them have come a long distance" (verses 2-3).

Jesus was putting a burden on the hearts of His disciples to love and serve the people by feeding them.

The disciples' reaction to Jesus' suggestion is classic: "But where in this remote place can anyone get enough bread to feed them?" (verse 4). All they could see was that they were in the desert and there wasn't any food nearby, and there were about 4000 hungry people in front of them. Jesus was asking the impossible!

Did they forget that they were talking with the One who had already done the impossible? Did they forget that in the past week or so He had healed a deaf and mute man, cast a demon out of a young girl, walked upon the water, calmed a storm by His presence and— get this—had *already fed about 5000 people* in another remote place no more than a couple weeks earlier with just five loaves and two fish?

I suppose they remembered all that when Jesus asked them, "How many loaves do you have?" (verse 5). I imagine they felt a bit sheepish when they answered "Seven!" (Could they have been thinking "Oh, man...remember what He did last time with just *five* loaves? And we have about 1000 fewer people here today!") You know the rest of the story. All the people were fed that day, and there were seven baskets of food left over.

That story of Jesus multiplying that food—and the disciples' insistence that it was impossible—is a reminder to us of how Jesus can take what little we have and make more than enough. That's what He did with Melissa's desire to help unwed mothers, even though she had limited resources. It's what He did with Pam's desire to serve the women in her church, even though she had little confidence and qualifications. It's what He'll do with *any* of us when He calls us to do something and we obey.

My friend Janice gave me a refrigerator magnet a couple years ago when I was struggling with doubts that God would provide all I needed to pursue my dream. The magnet read, "Where God guides, He provides." Sounds cliché, but it's so true. When He calls us to do something, He will provide all that we need to do it. Likewise, when He places a dream in your heart, my friend, He will give you all you need to reach it.

Esther's Example

The Bible is full of confidence-building stories about women who faced their calling alone and found God faithfully behind them, working out all the behind-the-scenes details so that His plan could ultimately be realized through them. My favorite one is the story of Esther.

Esther was a young Jewish woman who happened to be in the Persian king's harem at the time that a plot was concocted to annihilate all the Jews in Persia. Now Esther was an orphan who had been raised by her cousin, Mordecai, before going to live at the palace, and she was instructed by Mordecai to keep her nationality a secret. Talk about the least likely person being in the right place at the right time! I imagine Esther felt very alone in her big assignment the day Mordecai informed her that millions of Jewish people would be slaughtered within the month unless she figured out a way to use her position within the palace to stop the heinous plot. But who was she? A Jewish orphan with no prestigious background and no training in the skills of negotiation, no qualifications to persuade royalty, no earned reputation for credibility, and no status culturally as a woman. It was just her. Correction: It was just her and God.

Esther's actions at this time are worth noting. Her "strategy" before the intimidating king can be a strategy for any one of us who have dreams that may appear to loom larger than life or be slightly out of reach. Her boldness in carrying out God's plan for her life is an encouragement to any one of us who has ever felt alone in our dreams. So let's look at what this woman did when God called her to accomplish a very special task. (You might want to look at those ten short on-the-edge-of-your-seat chapters in the book of Esther to get the full story.)

She Considered the Calling

At first, Esther hesitated when her cousin told her to go before the king and ask that her people be spared. But when Mordecai implied that it wasn't just coincidence that an unlikely Jewish woman happened to have a position in the palace at the same time that an edict was made to slaughter all the Jews, Esther was cut to the core and convicted that perhaps she *was* in the palace "for such a time as this" (Esther 4:14).

That same phrase went through Pam's mind as well when she saw the potential for a women's ministry at her church and kept trying to push it out of her mind. Maybe she had been saved and burdened with a ministry for women "for such a time as this." I imagine Melissa, too, felt the burden of urgency, the calling on her life to open a home for the increasing number of single moms who needed help, and perhaps she, too, had felt she had been born "for such a time as this."

That confidence, that calling, that feeling that destiny might be hanging in the balance should cause *us* to move as well.

Now, sometimes when we have a dream in mind, or a burden we feel we must pursue or we're simply asked to do something, we have to figure out if it's just something *we'd* like to do, or something *someone else* would like us to do, or if it's something *God* is calling us to do. We can work through that question by asking:

1. *Is this something someone else can just as easily do?* If so, then maybe you're not necessarily being uniquely *called* to do it. All through our Christian lives, we will see opportunities to fulfill needs, and should help do so if we are able, along with fellow believers. Serving others should be a part of our lives, but such service won't necessarily be the same as a special calling.

2. *Is this something I have a strong heart's desire to do?* God generally calls us to an area that we would enjoy serving in, or that matches some of our natural abilities or areas of spiritual giftedness. For example, if you are easily annoyed by children, He's probably not calling *you* to teach that Sunday school class!

3. *Is this something I feel God prodding my heart to do?* Sometimes that conviction in our hearts simply won't go away, the need is very apparent, and no one else is stepping forward to meet it. When that happens, lift the matter to the Lord in prayer. If the burden persists, then it may be God's special calling.

When we take these questions to the Lord and say, "God, please confirm to me if I am the one to do this" and then wait for His answer, we can be more certain that we are *called* to something, and not just following our own desires or running in to rescue someone. (For more on discerning the dream God has placed on your heart see my book *When a Woman Discovers Her Dream* [Eugene, OR: Harvest House, 2005].)

She Gathered Prayer Support

Esther was quick to gather some serious prayer support. She immediately sent word to Mordecai to have all the Jews who were in that province pray for her and fast for three days, after which she was going to go before the king. Because her plan to go before the king uninvited could get her killed, I imagine her specific prayer request was, "Pray hard that God gives me the wisdom to know how to do this and to have the courage to see it through."

As a guideline for us, note that Esther didn't just ask people to pray that she be able to do something she had always wanted to do. In fact, she didn't want to do this at all, but she knew she had to follow the call God was placing on her life. The magnitude of her situation, and the thought that failure meant death for many people, caused her to realize that what she was up against was so big it was doomed to fail if she didn't keep God in it. So she gathered her most powerful ammunition: prayer.

I believe the reason Esther wanted prayer for her courage is because fear is the number-one obstacle that prevents us from pursuing our dreams. When people ask me to pray about their unfulfilled dreams, I pray using a 3-D approach: I ask God to give them the *discernment* to know if the dream is truly from Him; and if it is, I ask God to give them *direction* in how to pursue that dream, and to give them the *discipline* to actually do what God is calling them to do.

She Made a Plan and Carried It Out

Esther's task was an important one. I imagine she spent much time in prayer weighing out her options, or perhaps just sitting in silence begging God for anything resembling a plan! She evidently thought carefully, because eventually she came up with a very well thought-out plan.

Do you have a plan for accomplishing your dream as well? While God inspires and directs, He waits for you to follow through.

She Trusted in the Unseen

Esther's plan included twice holding a special banquet for the king and Haman, the evil man who wanted to exterminate the Jews. As Esther was carrying out her strategy of buttering up the king to be favorable to her request, God apparently was working behind the scenes to make the timing oh so perfect in every event that played out. (You have to read the entire story for yourself to fully appreciate just how perfect God's timing was!)

Esther must have realized at some point that as she did what she could, God would take care of the rest. That's exactly what He did. When the timing was right, Esther had the boldness of spirit to tell the king all about Haman's wicked plan and, in doing so, revealed that she, too, was Jewish and would be one of the people exterminated. That was enough for the king! After winning his heart with two scrumptious banquets, she now tells him that his right-hand man wants her and all her relatives, friends, and kinsmen dead! The king, angry at Haman, nullified the death order for the Jews, then ordered Haman to be executed on the very gallows that Haman had constructed the night before for Esther's cousin, Mordecai!

What's amazing about this story is the way God worked in the background to make things happen the way they did. Esther was God's willing servant, appointed by Him for a specific purpose at that time. God's calling on her life wasn't so much a dream as it was a prompting to be an instrument of His work. And as a result of following the call He placed on her heart, she became loved and praised throughout history and known as the queen who saved her people.

Answering the Call

What is the dream that God has placed in *your* heart? To go back to school and get your degree? To own your own business? To start a ministry that will encourage others? To fight for a cause that you know is right? Perhaps your dream is something as simple as making a difference in another person's life because of your faith and walk with God, or coming to see your neighbor or friend have the faith that you have. The same God who went before Esther goes before you. The same God who fed 4000 with seven loaves of bread still waits to multiply what you give Him.

Why? Because He is a God of grace. "And God is able to make *all* grace abound to you, so that in *all* things at *all* times, having *all* that you need, you will abound in *every* good work" (2 Corinthians 9:8, emphasis added). That doesn't leave much room for failure if you're walking in His will, does it?

So, go for it, my friend, and take Psalm 18:28-29 with you as your God-confidence: "You, O LORD, keep my lamp burning...with your help I can advance against a troop; with my God I can scale a wall."

What do you need God-confidence to go up against? Is God big enough to help you know success? What wall is obstructing you from accomplishing your dream? Is God big enough to help you leap over it? You bet!

Begin counting on Him to keep your lamp burning. He's the One who parted the seas, brought city walls down flat, changed the hearts of kings, and raised a Savior from the dead. Surely there is nothing beyond His ability to do through *you!*

Pursuing Your Dream

For Personal Application

1. What are some things you've longed to do for God that you have been hesitant to try?

Will you release the responsibility from those who have not supported you in your dream and realize that if God wants you to accomplish it, He will enable you to do it? Begin praying for *discernment* as to whether it's truly His will, and if that seems to be the case, then ask for *direction* for how to go about it and then the *discipline* to see it through.

2. Perhaps you've never thought about the idea of God placing a dream in your heart. If not, begin praying daily that God would show you what He has purposed for you. A good way to pray is to say, "Lord, burden my heart with the things that burden Your heart." Then pray that He will accomplish in and through you His plans for your life.

3. Find some confidence-building verses in your Bible and mark the ones that speak to you about the dream God has placed in your heart. (You can start with the ones that are mentioned in this chapter.) Write a date and a couple of words next to the verses in your Bible that remind you of the "dream" He has given you. By marking these verses in your Bible, it will soon become your promise book and your confidence when it comes to pursuing your dream.

4. Find a trusted friend to pray the 3-D approach for you (discernment, direction, and discipline), and ask that friend to hold you accountable for that last "D."

For Further Study

Read the following verses and prayerfully respond to them as they speak to you concerning the dream God has placed on your heart.

Exodus 14:14:

Psalm 18:28-29:

Psalm 37:4-5:

Psalm 84:11:

2 Corinthians 9:8:

Philippians 4:13:

With Esther 4:14 in mind, what area of your life might God be using you "for such a time as this"? (Remember, a "dream" God places on your heart is not simply about you and your happiness, but about Him and what He wants to accomplish through you. It's possible there may be a difficult or even uncomfortable element about a dream God has whispered upon your heart—primarily so He can prove to others that He is the One who can do the work through you.)

Alone in Serving:
RELATING TO THE HEART OF JESUS

s a single mother, Gail saw God come through for her many times. He provided for her and her children, brought unexpected joys into her life, and even gave her a new husband who loved her and her children as his own. But Gail didn't expect the feelings of aloneness to rush in again when she stepped out to minister to other women who were where she once was. In fact, forging a ministry for single moms was almost as difficult as being a single mom all over again.

Out of a desire to minister to other single moms because of how God had ministered to her, Gail founded SMORE for Women (Single Moms Overjoyed, Rejuvenated, Empowered!), an alliance of compassionate women whose goal is to encourage single moms to reach their full potential.[1] The organization started in 2007 and she now has a board of 10 women representing seven different denominations and a blog with hundreds of followers. She also offers a weekly Bible class for single moms in her church, a yearly retreat open to all single moms, and a Day of Blessing, in which she comes to a church by appointment and serves, blesses, and encourages single moms in a day of pampering.

"I have a great passion for what I'm doing; I believe in it," Gail said. "Yet sometimes I feel like I'm beating my head against the wall to get the church, as a whole, to recognize the need for this ministry. I feel like a prophet in the wilderness trying to convince people of this huge need that can make an enormous impact on generations."

∾

As a director of women's ministries, Cyndi also knows what it's like to feel alone while serving. She knew she was called to serve the women in her church. She longed to see them connect with God and each other. But why was it so difficult to find women to help lead Bible studies, serve on a planning team for a women's event, or even commit to participating in activities or a program designed to help grow their soul? Cyndi knew God was going before her. Yet she still felt so alone.

"When planning a conference, a monthly or quarterly fellowship, or even a fun weekend retreat it seems there are few who want to commit or even participate," Cyndi said. "I end up calling or approaching women when I see them to try to convince them that they need to come. They seem to resist allowing themselves the enjoyment of an evening out or some time away. I have often wondered if we, as women in the church, have missed the mark somehow in intentionally connecting with each other in small-group study and in worship times, leaving a void in which we don't sense connection, inclusion, or value."

∾

And as the wife of a senior pastor, Sue has heard many heartbreaking stories from those who have been abandoned, mistreated, misunderstood, or involved in a secret, sinful lifestyle.

"The stories that unfold are those that cannot be shared with others, so my husband and I often will carry these burdens alone," Sue said. "For me it is personally challenging when I hear the tragic stories during the week and later see the hurting people on Sunday, knowing what they are going through. Sometimes it feels like we're the only ones who know the painful truth behind the smiles."

Our Expectations in Serving

Have you ever felt like any of those women? If so, you are not alone.

To follow our Lord into a place of ministry means allowing Him to mold and shape our character to be more like His own. But the molding and shaping can be painful at times. And, except for the faithful companionship of our God, who walks alongside us through this process, we can also feel very alone. Sometimes we even get the notion that we should be immune from hardships—or at least the feeling of being alone. After all, when we're serving, we're right where God wants us to be, so our lives should be filled with blessings, right? Actually, it's when we're depending on God and His strength to get us through that we are right where we need to be. That means God will allow into our lives and ministries whatever it takes to keep us dependent on Him. Whether you serve in an official ministry capacity or not, any time you step out to serve or invest your life in another, you are making yourself vulnerable to being hurt. But you are also putting yourself in a position where God can draw you closer to His heart.

We also tend to think that when we walk through a door of service that God opens for us there will only be pleasant pastures and continual success. Yet ministry is often where God prunes us and makes us more like Himself. In John 15:2, Jesus said His Father, the Vinedresser, "cuts off every branch in me that bears no fruit, while *every branch that does bear fruit he prunes so that it will be even more fruitful*" (emphasis added). That means those frustrations you encounter, the hurts you receive, the painful "shaping of your character" are all a part of God's pruning process so you will be even more effective in your service for Him. Feelings of frustration or aloneness are part of the pruning processes God has often used in my own life as I've become comfortable—and sometimes even stagnant—in the course of serving Him.

His Expectations of Us

While we have certain expectations of what our life of service should look like, God has expectations, as well.

God's plan is to make us more like His Son, no matter what it takes. And serving others definitely makes us more like Him. We are told in Scripture to consider it joy when we encounter various trials because the testing of our faith produces endurance (James 1:2-3). And we are encouraged through Scripture that "in all things God works for the good of those who love him, who have been called according to his purpose." The next verse tells us why we can be encouraged: "For those God foreknew he also predestined to be conformed to the likeness of his Son" (Romans 8:28-29). Making us more like Jesus, not necessarily our success in ministry, is God's goal for our lives.

How Ministry Molds Us

As we seek to grow closer to Christ by serving Him, we sometimes fail to realize that the difficulties, the frustrations, and the aloneness we encounter can be used by God to bring us closer to Christ and make us more like Him. Oh, my friend, as you step out to serve God and others, you are walking into a precious opportunity for character development.

There are two key ways that ministry molds our character and makes us more like Christ.

1. Ministry to Others Helps Us Relate to the Heart of Jesus

My friend, Jini, has been able to relate to the heart of Jesus through hurtful situations, misunderstandings, and false accusations.

"Once in a while, as a pastor's wife I have been falsely accused of something when it came to my actions or more commonly, my motives. It always feels bad when that happens, but I have been able to go to Jesus and cry out to Him and ponder the times that He had been falsely accused during His ministry on earth. That has saved me from lashing out or defending myself in ways that I know will not bring glory to God. He soothes my soul and I relish being able to 'share' something in common with Him."

I too have had situations in which being hurt by others has led me straight to Christ's heart. For example, one woman in our church had a long history of her family being helped, encouraged, and ministered to. She was a sweet, caring person. I considered her my friend. And I didn't expect to hear from her what I did one Sunday morning.

She said she felt she wasn't connecting with anyone and she didn't feel like our church was her home. "We won't be a part of this church family anymore," she said as she left that morning. Her words stung. (And as the senior pastor's wife, that kind of comment cuts deeper than any other.)

I stood in the church parking lot in disbelief as she drove off, wondering what *more* could have been done for her and her family to feel connected, supported, and loved. Then I got into my car and started the drive for home. That's when the anger inside of me began to surface.

"God I'm *tired* of this," I cried aloud. "I poured my heart into her…this church helped her and her family through all sorts of hardships. We prayed for her, stood by her, bailed her out financially. And this is the thanks we get? She's getting up and leaving because she doesn't feel she *connected* with anyone? God, I'm so tired of being hurt by people I'm just trying to love and serve."

As soon as I said those words, my heart was convicted. I sensed the Lord's voice as if He were saying, "Do you think I've never felt that way?"

I realized then that although this woman said her farewell to me, she was walking out on Christ. It was *His* church, not mine. It was *His* love and encouragement, through us, that she was rejecting. She was walking away from the family *He* had placed her in. His wounds ran deeper than mine that day. His wounds always have.

Just knowing that Jesus shared that pain with me, that He understood, that He felt it before I did, reinforced to me that I was not alone. And realizing that I myself have hurt God in many of the same ways gave me a renewed motivation that day to continue serving others (even if some walk away), and to continue pouring out my heart (even if some don't give back) simply because my Lord has continued to do that for me.

When I realized I shared that wound with Jesus that day, I saw clearer into *His* wounds. And to this day, it is a precious memory of having shared a moment with Christ. I wouldn't even call it sharing in the *sufferings* of Christ, since what I went through isn't anywhere near what He has suffered on my behalf. In fact it wasn't suffering at all. It was only heartache over a lost friend, a sense of betrayal, but it was something my Lord experienced many times. And it was a small price to pay to be called His follower and His servant.

2. Ministry to Others Forces Us to Rely on God Alone

Mary, a friend of mine with a tender heart for others, shared with me her frustrations in ministry that have helped her come to know a closer intimacy with her Lord.

- I have felt alone when I have asked for help in a ministry and no one responds.

- I have felt alone when a scheduled meeting is poorly attended or everyone cancels at the last minute.

- I have felt alone when everyone leaves a function and I'm left alone to do the cleanup work.

- I have felt alone when I have no one to call or meet with to share a ministry challenge or prayer need.

- I have felt alone when I have tried to share a discouragement or time of loneliness and there is no real connection or understanding.

- I have felt alone when I am misunderstood and have had nowhere to turn.

- I have felt alone when there is a lack of visible results in ministry and I wonder whether the ministry is making a difference.

Yet Mary admits these frustrations and alone times in ministry have increased her dependence on and her intimacy with God.

"God has used the lonely times in my life as times of personal growth—times that have made me run to Him for strength and understanding," Mary said. "I have had sweet times with the Lord, during which He has provided peace and comfort and encouragement."

As she looks back on her frustrations in ministry, she is able to say,

- In loneliness, I have learned to be able to let go of a service passion if the support is not there.
- In loneliness, I have realized that my ideas of service are not always in line with God's will and timing.
- In loneliness, I have grown in my reliance on God for my needs.
- In loneliness, I have learned to turn to God in prayer.
- In loneliness, I have learned to confess bitterness and not let it take root in my heart.
- In loneliness, I have learned to confess wrong attitudes and reflect upon any sin that may be hindering a blessing.
- In loneliness, I have learned to trust in God's timing and purpose for ministry goals.
- In loneliness, I have learned to trust that God is at work even if I don't see the results.
- In loneliness, I have enjoyed personal times with God and His assurance of love and acceptance.
- In loneliness, I have grown in my compassion for others.

A wealth of intimacy with God comes when we feel alone in serving. I wonder if that is just as important to God's heart as our actual service. He is interested in what we *become*, not just what we actually *do*.

Jesus' Dependence on God Alone

Jesus faced many frustrations in ministry as His disciples struggled to display the kind of faith He expected of them. At times Jesus was tired, worn out by the crowds. It was then that He sought alone times with His heavenly Father to rejuvenate His soul.

Jesus left us the example from His own life of fully depending on His Father to nurture His soul and give Him the strength He needed to continue His mission. Yet we sometimes feel that if we simply surround ourselves with others, we will be strong. It's difficult sometimes to go straight to God or His Word, so we look to someone we can relate to on a human level. Sometimes we even look to one person to be our spiritual giant or champion. While it is good to have mentors in our lives and women we can look up to, spiritually, we must never let them replace God in our lives. It's all too easy for us to enthrone spiritual champions in our lives, but when that happens, we have placed our dependence on people, rather than God. And we are in danger of being gravely disappointed, or experiencing the feeling of abandonment that inevitably happens when those people fade out of our lives.

In his beloved classic *My Utmost for His Highest,* Oswald Chambers warns:

A servant of God must stand so very much alone that he never realizes he is alone. In the early stages of the Christian life, disappointments will come—people who used to be lights will flicker out, and those who used to stand with us will turn away. We have to get so used to it that we will not even realize we are standing alone...We must build our faith not on fading lights but on the Light that never fails. When "important" individuals go away we are sad, until we see that they are meant to go, so that only one thing is left for us to do—to look into the face of God for ourselves. [2]

When we are serving, we will find ourselves in situations where there is no one we can really talk to, no one who understands, no one who can go with us to a certain place. That is the time when we are sweetly reminded that we are learning a reliance on God alone.

Pressing On for the Prize

So how does it become a little less painful? How can we begin to feel a little less lonely as we serve God and others? By keeping our perspective about what Jesus requires of us and what we must be willing to do to continue to grow stronger (and more like Him) through the seasons of life.

1. Remember that Jesus Faced Frustrating Times Too

Hebrews 4:15 says that Jesus, as our High Priest, can sympathize with our weaknesses and all we go through because He has been tempted in all things as we are, yet He was without sin. On those days when you feel you are the only one who has experienced something hurtful, or you feel like giving up because of how you've been treated, or you feel like telling someone off out of your anger, remember that Jesus has walked in your shoes…and He has paved the way so it's a bit easier for you to endure.

Jesus faced disappointments, especially when it came to dealing with people. Even those closest to Him let Him down numerous times. For example:

- When His disciples were freaking out in a storm while He was right there in the boat with them, He asked: "Why are you so afraid? Do you still have no faith?" (Mark 4:40).

- After Jesus miraculously fed the 5000, walked on water, and then fed another 4000, He rebuked His disciples, saying, "Why are you talking about having no bread? Do you still not see or understand? Are your hearts hardened? Do you have eyes but fail to see, and ears but fail to hear? And don't you remember? When I broke the five loaves for the five thousand, how many basketfuls of pieces did you pick up?…And when I broke the seven loaves for the four thousand, how many basketfuls of pieces did you pick up?…Do you still not understand?" (Mark 8:17-21).

- When a man complained to Jesus that His disciples could not drive out an evil spirit from his demon-possessed son, Jesus replied, "O unbelieving generation, how long shall I be with you? How long shall I put up with you?" (Mark 9:17-19 NASB).

Yet Jesus did not give up on His disciples. He continued to invest in them, shaping and molding their character and instilling in them what they would need so they could eventually "turn the world upside down" (Acts 17:6 KJV).

Scripture encourages us to not give up—to keep our eyes on Jesus, "the author and finisher of our faith, who for the joy set before him endured the cross" (Hebrews 12:2).[3] When people disappoint you, let you down, or simply don't get it like you wish they would, remember that Jesus experienced all that too.

2. Rely on God for Your Strength to Continue

My mother, Joyce, has been in ministry most of her life. After more than 50 years of serving in the church, she is convinced that Jesus knew what He was talking about when He said, "Apart from me, you can do nothing" (John 15:5).

"The longer I serve, the more I realize I have no ability apart from God's enablement. As a worship leader, if ever I've dared to face a congregation while drawing on my own wisdom or experience, it has been one of the worst Sundays ever! Even as an accomplished pianist, if ever I thought I could rely on my own skills to play a meaningful solo, I'd fail completely. I'm now very aware that in order to do or be for God's glory in any public ministry, 'He must increase, but I must decrease' (John 3:30 NASB). I've learned through experience that the key to being used by God is to be in the Word and in *prayer* to God."

If Jesus required alone times with His father to nourish His soul, regain perspective, and regain strength to complete His mission, how much more do we need to rely on God for the same? When I begin to feel misunderstood, unappreciated, alone, or overwhelmed, it usually means I have neglected personal time with the Lord to keep my soul in check. Or, I've become so accustomed to success in my own power that God lets me experience a little "success" on my own, and then I get my wake-up call!

That happened recently when I planned a women's conference at my church—the largest conference I'd ever planned on the largest budget I've ever worked with. I'd never lost money on a conference, and have never had weak attendance, so I was feeling pretty confident—in myself. However, when the registrations started coming in very slowly, I began wondering what was wrong. I asked myself, "Did I really pray about this? Did I weigh it carefully before God to see if He wanted this? Did I get the approval of my team?"

Then I began to ask the Lord some questions: "God, did I read You wrong on this one? Did I run ahead of You because I wanted it more than You did?" As I shared my doubts with my leadership team, they assured me that we did decide, together, to go forward with the conference. But I was in the mind-set of thinking, *I have to make it happen*, rather than trusting God and acknowledging that *He's* the only One who could make it happen.

And that's what God did. When I finally thrust the whole plan and project at His feet and said, "I can't do this... I will pull the plug on this if You want me to, but just don't let me walk through this alone," that is when the registrations began to pour in. It was as if God was waiting for me to admit to Him that I was powerless so He could show me where the power was and who was ultimately in control.

Think about it. When we rely on strength other than God's, that is when we begin to notice that His power is gone. Far be it from me to try to do *anything* in my own power.

3. Refuse to Run Out Ahead of Him

That experience taught me to wait on God before rushing into my own plans. After all, Jesus consulted with His Father before He did anything. Our tendency is to see a need and rush to meet it without prayerfully considering whether or not that is where God wants us to serve.

My friend, Chris, often feels alone in ministry when she feels she's the only one aware of certain needs and steps in to meet them without the help of others. But those are the times she stops and asks herself, *Am I rushing in to rescue this person in my own power, or is God leading the way on this?*

Sometimes we get so busy that we stop taking the time to pray for God's input. We have a million irons in the fire, and we're stretched to the limit, so we feel alone and say, "Why isn't anyone helping me? Why are *You* not helping me, God?" But the reality of the situation might be that we've run ahead of God and we are out there "by ourselves" in a manner of speaking, waiting for God to catch up with us.

My friend, Deb, a women's ministry director whose husband is a leader in her church as well, says she at times feels like giving up. And she realizes that's usually an indication of her heart condition and that she needs more alone time with God.

"On those days when I feel like giving up, I just need to surrender to Him. I try to take as much time as I can to be still, and ask Him for rest and guidance. Some days, my wanting to give up is mostly about me. I am tired, burned out, or feeling like I need to do it all alone. He points that [self-reliant mind-set] out to me, and that I just need to be obedient and listen!"

I've been known to "rescue" in ministry, too, rather than wait upon God to see if I am the one who needs to respond. I've done this particularly in the area of discipleship. I love nothing more than to see a woman grow spiritually, grasp truths and biblical insights, and make them her own, and then begin discipling other women as well. But there are probably more women who flounder along the way, making wrong choices, than women who have not. In retrospect I've had to ask myself, *Was she ready for what I expected of her? Had she come to the place where she was ready to surrender, or did I assume that of her, force that upon her, or push her through a door that God had not yet prepared her heart for? Was I more zealous for her spiritual growth than she was?*

In recent years, I have disciplined myself to wait upon the Lord in prayer to show me who I should pour myself into. I want His choice for me—not to run out and try to convince every woman whose path I cross that they need to be discipled. Jesus tarried in prayer all night before selecting 12 followers to pour His life into. Why should I assume I need to do less?

When we run out ahead of God, we'll end up serving in our own power. But when we wait on Him, He will equip us with all we need to get the job done.

4. Render to Him Your Losses as a Loving Sacrifice

It's easy for us to offer our victories to Christ and say, "This I did for You." There can even be a hint of pride in that…as we tend to think we succeeded in some way for the kingdom. *(Lord, I brought that woman to a saving knowledge of You. Lord, I planned that event and many lives were changed for You. Lord, aren't You proud of me?)*

But how many times do we offer our failures to Him and say, "This I did for You" with just as sincere a heart? I must admit that the times I've sensed the most comfort and closeness to the Lord have been when I was deeply hurt in ministry, either from something I didn't do too well, or from a situation in which I tried my best but didn't get the results I had hoped for. Whether it was a women's event I poured my heart into and only a handful of women showed up, or a woman I discipled who, after several months of guidance, turned and walked away, it is still an offering to the Lord. God takes not only what we see as our successes, but the things we deem failures as well. He uses them all to make us humble and more like Himself.

My friend, Barbara, said even the weak moments in her life have become a precious offering to God, and the fact that He can use those moments still amazes her.

"When I know that I'm not 'on my game' so to speak—when I'm distracted, dry, and weary, He works things out," she said. "At my lowest, when I feel the most unworthy, He ministers through me. I'm always amazed after the fact. He just wants us to be obedient and say yes, or, as I say, show up. And He speaks to the hearts of those He sends to me. So I stand in awe that He would use me in spite of my sorry, shabby self."

It's when we feel we are sorry and shabby that God sometimes uses us the most. When we are feeling good about ourselves, we are tempted to minister in our own strength and we end up being powerless. But when we are feeling shabby and unworthy, that is when Christ is strong through us. As the apostle Paul said, "When I am weak [in myself], then I am strong [in Christ]" (2 Corinthians 12:10).

5. Realize We Serve Him to Be Obedient, Not to See Results

You and I may not see the results of our work while we're here on earth. We may disciple other women and not live to see them turn their world around. We may pour out our hearts into helping that woman in her marital struggles and still see her walk away from her marriage. We may continue to be the unnoticed woman in the back of the church office, stuffing the Sunday bulletins, or rocking the cranky baby in the nursery, or cleaning the fellowship hall after the event. But there is One who walks alongside us, notices our efforts, and smiles as He quietly says, "Well done, My good and faithful servant."

God simply calls us to be faithful, and we are to leave the results in His hands.

When Your Cup Overflows

If I ended this chapter talking only about the frustrations and aloneness of ministry, I would be misrepresenting to you the joy of a servant of God. Yes, there are times when you will feel alone while serving. Yes, there are times you will feel disappointed, frustrated, and ready to give up. But there are also days (and prayerfully, you'll experience many of these) when you will realize there is nothing more fulfilling on earth—nothing you would rather be doing with your life—than serving Him.

At the beginning of this chapter, we heard the cries of women who felt alone in ministry. Now listen to their songs of praise to the One who makes it all worth it.

Partnering in Kingdom Work

Mary, who shared earlier of her growing reliance upon God as a result of her alone times in ministry, said that what keeps her going is not just the fear of being outside God's will, but the knowledge that "the blessings in the end are too wonderful to miss."

She shared with me one of those blessings that she keeps as a polished gem in her heart to remind her that even the lowliest and most frustrating of tasks done for the kingdom of God are worth it:

"For the past ten years, I have been a group leader for a large area women's conference. I had committed to bringing a group of 50 to this conference, and it had been a challenge from the start to get the commitments and collect payment from the women who indicated their interest in attending. Many times during the process I said to the Lord, 'I'm done. This is the last year I am doing this, Lord.' After we got to the event and all the planning and work was done, the blessings started to pour in as I saw and heard the women laugh and connect with each other and enjoy the weekend.

"The greatest moment of the event was when my aunt filled out the response card indicating that she had received Christ as Savior at the conference. I felt so much joy that I immediately said in my heart, 'It was all worth it.' And I remember thinking later that no amount of work could ever compare to the joy of being a part of God's plan of salvation for someone. In addition, when we returned from the conference, my father—the brother of my aunt—said some wonderful words of encouragement to me that I will always cherish."

God doesn't have to give us sweet glimpses of the rewards of our service, but every so often He does. I see that as His tender grace in action, offering us a bit of encouragement that will inspire us to keep going. A glimpse here, a word there, a story we happen to hear years later that helps us put the pieces together and say, "God, You *did* work something glorious out of what I thought was for nothing." In fact, every time God allows me a glimpse of what He's doing or has done, I can't help but fall in love with Him all over again and gain a new appreciation for what He is able to do in *His* way and in *His* time.

Seeing God's Grace in Your Own Life

My mentor, Barbara, said that her "aha moment" of realizing the alone times in ministry are worth it is when she realizes God was really ministering to her during the time she was ministering to someone else.

"I realize it was all worth it when I walk away and it occurs to me that God had me minister to that person because He wanted me to hear what I was telling them, for my own edification or encouragement. How amazing that He speaks to me through my ministry to others."

Finding Jesus as Your Treasure

Jini, my friend who is a pastor's wife and has learned to relate to Jesus through times of being falsely accused or misunderstood, talks of the precious Word of God as her reason to never give up, no matter how tiring or frustrating ministry can be.

"Really, the bottom line in what helps me to never give up is God's Word. Seeing Jesus and His Word as my treasure has made all the difference in my life. The man in the parable of the hidden treasure went out and with joy gave away everything he had so he could obtain the treasure. Knowing how God views Himself in our lives helps me immeasurably when things get tough. I can 'feel' all I want like giving up, but I know better because of the wonder of it all as found in His Word— the wonder of being obedient and living out His call on our lives."

Jini, whose husband started a church in Utah to help people see the truth of Jesus Christ and His Word, has seen many times that the aloneness and frustrations in ministry are truly worthwhile.

"We hold 'pastor's desserts' in our home every five weeks or so," Jini said. "All new people from our church are invited to come and ask questions and tell their story. I can be completely exhausted in ministry and yet those evenings thrill my soul and remind me that it is all worth it as I hear about the stirrings of life-change in someone's life. To see that our little efforts are used by the God of the universe and His power to cause someone to actually begin a journey toward His heart is like pressing the reset button of my soul!"

Remembering His Faithfulness

My mother, Joyce, who has served in various aspects of church ministry all her life, has served many of those years while enduring chronic back pain. And after more than 50 years of serving God, even when it hurts, she says, "Of course there have been times when I just wanted to chuck it all! But when I think of God's impeccable faithfulness toward me, I feel compelled to serve Him with everything He's given me. I'm energized by knowing His call on my life and sensing His smile on my obedience. I'm most fulfilled when I'm busy for Christ. That makes me press on."

Recognizing God At Work

Gail, who admits that ministry among single moms doesn't often produce visible results, has learned to recognize the little ways God is at work—in the life of one woman at a time. A precious comment, a song dedicated and sung to her, a thank-you note in the mail—God always gives her just what she needs to know that her work is not for nothing. And by faith, she presses on, knowing God is at work whether she sees it or not.

Experiencing Joy and Peace

Cyndi, the women's ministry director, says that the things she has gained by serving her Lord don't compare to any frustrations she has encountered along the way.

"I have experienced joy in humility by being used in another's life and seeing real change happen that only God can do through broken vessels. And I have experienced sweet peace in freedom by serving with no pretense. He has shown me how to move in peace and joy through whatever venue He ordains. I am learning to serve out of love for Christ alone and not to let people steal this joy. Serving out of love for Christ brings no disappointment."

Sensing His Smile

And Sue, the pastor's wife, sums up the incredible fulfillment that comes as we see others growing closer to God simply because we were available to serve in whatever way He called us.

In Sue's counseling ministry, God has brought along a few women who have become dear friends who have let her know how God has used her to speak to them.

"Sometimes after hearing their positive reports, I'll think to myself, *Did I say all that?* It truly is worth it all when I find out how God has used my feeble attempts in spite of my inadequacies. Their discouragement, their depression, has been traded in for a peace and joy that goes beyond human understanding. I can spend hours with someone with very little to show for it, but the women who help to put the wind back in my sails are those who have grabbed ahold of God and His Word and have renewed their minds and transformed their hearts to be more like Jesus."

Yes, serving feels lonely at times. Ministry can be frustrating when we don't see immediate results or we are stumbling through the pruning process God is allowing in our lives. But there is joy in being obedient to God. And there is strength for those who rely on God to get them through.

So What Are You Waiting For?

God calls each of us to minister in one way or another. As He lays it on your heart to step out and serve on His behalf, He will equip you, empower you, and walk alongside you at all times—including the days you feel you can't give one ounce more. And as you place your full dependence upon Him and walk in His footsteps by serving others, you too will experience His strength, hope, and joy.

Serve boldly, my friend. You are not alone.

Alone in Serving

For Personal Application

1. What frustrations have made you feel like retreating from a ministry position or from serving others?

2. How have these frustrations or disappointments given you an opportunity to become more like Christ?

3. In what way have disappointments, hurts, or "failures" in ministry helped you relate more to the heart of Jesus?

4. Is there any hurt that you can now offer up to God and say, "This I did for You"? Remember, He cares about the "failures" as much as the successes. It is your heart that He wants to shape, not necessarily a successful ministry.

5. Spend some time in prayer, and rededicate your heart to the Lord for service. Remember that you serve not to be happy and successful, but to be obedient. If God knows your heart is intent on obeying Him, He will care for it and recharge it for continued service.

For Further Study

Read Jesus' words in John 15:1-12.

What does Jesus say happens to every branch that bears fruit (verse 2)?

What is God's intended result from this pruning?

What are we to do as He is pruning us (verse 4)?

What are two results of our abiding in Him (verses 5-7)?

What is the benefit to God of our abiding in Him (verse 8)?

How can we continue to abide in Him (verse 10)?

What is our ultimate reward for abiding in Him, even during the pruning process (verse 11)?

Finally, what are we commanded to do in spite of any hurts we may feel during the pruning process (verse 12)?

Considering God's words and your answers above, write a prayer to God. Tell Him all that is on your mind as you continue to serve Him, and consider new ways you can serve.

Alone with Your God:
LIVING IN HIS ABUNDANCE

*T*he hum of the engines caused a lump to swell in my throat. As the plane started moving slowly toward the runway, I leaned my head against the window in the rear seat of the airplane and fought back tears.

Why do I have to feel so alone—why now? I thought.

I was flying across the country for a television interview and should have felt confident and excited. But instead, my heart was aching over an unresolved argument between my husband and myself the night before. My pride told me to wait until *he* said he was sorry. But as I was waiting for those words, he fell asleep...and I ended up leaving the house before dawn in order to catch my flight. The thought of flying across the country with a hole in my heart made me nauseous. *He knows I hate to leave if everything is not right with us,* I thought. My hurt began to swell with anger.

I knew I could call Hugh at my first layover (which is what I ended up doing). But it would be three days before we could talk again, and not until then could I have a reassuring hug. Just knowing that intensified my feelings of loneliness.

As the plane raced down the runway and prepared to lift off, I felt that familiar tugging at my heart. I ignored the flight attendant's instructions to keep all carry-on items stowed securely beneath my seat and I grabbed my Bible and flipped it open to Luke 15, where my bookmark happened to be from my reading the morning before. I read, quickly, the story of the prodigal son. *This doesn't relate to me*, I thought bitterly. Then I read it again, keeping in mind that Jesus told this story to teach us about our heavenly Father's love. I stopped at the conversation between the father and his older son, who was jealous that his rebellious younger brother was getting so much attention upon returning home. The father's gentle rebuke toward his older son pierced my heart: "My son," the father said, "you are always with me, and everything I have is yours" (verse 31).

All that He has is mine.

In that moment, as the plane lifted off the ground, I settled into the realization that I am always with Him, no matter how far I might feel from anyone else. As the plane gained altitude, I sensed my Father's loving arms around me, carrying me on His wings to a place where nothing could hurt my heart again. I closed my eyes and thought about those gentle words—"everything I have is yours"— and gained strength in knowing that I had *all* of His compassion, *all* of His understanding, *all* of His peace, and *all* of His unfailing love. As I drifted above the clouds, I realized this was one of those "alone times" when I felt right next to His heart…and there was no other place on earth I wanted to be.

Since that day, I have come to realize that it is in the times that we feel truly alone that we often sense God's presence most powerfully. Now, that doesn't mean God's presence lessens any at the times we're not alone—He is always with us at all times. But it's interesting how, in moments of true aloneness we come to realize we have no other resource to turn to but God—and for that reason, the alone times in life can be a good thing for us.

Are you finding by now that your times of aloneness compel you to draw closer to God's heart? Are you recalling some of your intense alone times and how they possibly allowed Him to penetrate that place in your heart and fill you with Himself? Hopefully by now you can see that only the unfailing love of God—in our most desperately alone times—can fulfill us, can give us what we truly need…and cause us to actually *long* to be alone—with Him.

Longing to Be with Him

Catherine remembers that feeling of longing to be away from everyone else and alone with her God. She had just lost her husband, Ray, a few days earlier. Upon leaving the room where his lifeless body lay, she remembers praying, "Lord, You be my Husband now. You be my Protector and my Defender and my Strength and my Shield. And Lord, help me to grieve quickly, and let it not overwhelm me."

"I invited God into that place in my life that my husband had occupied, and when I went out that door, He went with me. And I have never felt alone."

But she has, since then, felt very much like she *wanted* to be alone…with her God.

At Ray's memorial service and afterward, people clamored around her, stayed with her, waited on her, not wanting her to be by herself. Yet she felt that pressing urge to have everyone leave so she could be alone with God.

"I thought, *If everyone would just leave, I can start this grieving process and I can start my alone time with God.* They meant well, wanting to be my comfort, but I wanted God's comfort, and that happens when you're alone with Him."

Catherine eventually got her alone time with God, grieved the loss of her husband, and saw the faithfulness of God in how she was able to grieve quickly and thoroughly and never feel that the rivers of grief had swept over her.

It's now been nearly 13 years since Catherine lost Ray. But she has never felt that loneliness that comes from missing a husband, only a deepening of her communion with God. "Of course I miss Ray, and at times I miss being married, but now I can do things I never could before." Some of her new joy came in discovering who she was during her alone times with God. She was not just Ray's wife, but a woman much loved by God.

"I still want my friends around and I still enjoy being with people, but there's a deepening joy that comes with being alone with God. Because of that, I look forward to being alone. I enjoy it. It's not *loneliness*, like I'm in despair and lacking something. It's *aloneness*, like when I'm in a deeper state with God."

You'd have to look into Catherine's eyes and see that sparkle to get a glimpse of the joy she now experiences alone with her God. Catherine has found her Oasis in a season of life that most would call a desert.

Finding Your Oasis

Have you found *your* Oasis as well? I know you started this journey with me in the desert as we looked at being alone as a woman, a wife, and a mother. You learned to lift your head as we looked at how God meets us when we're alone in our pain. You gained a deeper trust in Him as we looked at being alone in our spiritual life and in worship. And you got a new focus as we looked at being alone in our trials, alone in our restlessness, and alone in pursuing our dreams. I hope that by now you have come to "taste and see that the LORD is good" (Psalm 34:8), and that the deserts in life He allows you to walk through can be doorways to a deeper intimacy with Him. And I hope by now you can say you have walked *through* your desert of emptiness to a place of abundance, an oasis of strength in Him.

The dictionary defines an oasis as a fertile spot in a desert made possible by the presence of water. It's that source of refreshment that springs up in a dry and barren place, it's that pool of peace that we camp out next to so we'll never thirst again. It's also a place where things grow, in the midst of things that have wilted away. I love that picture. And I love how God becomes that Source of Refreshment to us not only in His unfailing love and His constant presence, but in the way He causes us to grow and bloom and flourish as we stick next to Him.

Reaping the Benefits

Before we end our journey together, I want to encourage you by pointing out some benefits of our alone times—some ways that God enables us to grow as we camp next to His stream that never runs dry. Most likely you will recognize some of these "benefits to being alone with God" as strengths in your life already...evidence that God is indeed working within you and causing you to grow and bloom in the deserts of life. I encourage you to see this list of benefits as a check-list of what God has already done in your life or a hope chest of what you have to look forward to as He continues to mold you into the woman of strength that you were designed to be.

We Learn to Depend *on God*

There is a true joy and liberty that comes from not depending on our husbands, self-help books, counselors, friends, circumstances, material things, or even the church when we feel alone. There is a special confidence we gain when we say, like David says in Psalm 62, "My soul waits in silence for God only...He only is my rock and my salvation" (verses 1-2 NASB). There's a transformation that happens in that waiting on Him alone, as Julia testifies. Julia, whose stories of aloneness are told in the first few chapters of this book, experienced her most intense alone times after her 20-year-old daughter was killed in a car explosion. Dealing with that has taught her, more than anything else, what it means to depend on God and wait for Him.

"Dealing with that kind of grief is definitely an alone thing," Julia said. "Not even family members can help because they have their own grief, and each person handles it differently. I went to grief recovery and read all the books. But only the Lord was able to comfort me or bring me any peace. At times it has also been helpful to talk to someone who is sensitive and will listen. My major breakthroughs, however, have come as the result of other Christians praying specifically for my pain and through my extended times of silence and solitude with the Lord."

Wouldn't you agree that those times when no one else can help us are the times we learn what it really means to depend on the Lord?

We Discover *Who We Really Are*

When we get away from others and sit before God alone, our hearts and minds and true personalities are laid bare before Him—and us. This can sometimes be disturbing (which is why many of us don't like to be alone), but it can be healing and refreshing, too, as God reveals to us who we are in His eyes, not ours and everyone else's.

Vickie discovered this recently. During an alone time in her life, she attended a women's event in which they were asked to cut up magazines and make a collage representing themselves. At first she thought the assignment was silly, and that it was some sort of New Age "self-discovery" activity. "But I ended up having a ball," she said. "As I started cutting up magazines, I began to realize that I am not just Lee's wife. I'm a woman of God, I'm a good mother, I'm someone who loves music and nature and beauty." After creating that collage and recognizing more about who she was from the inside out, Vickie said she gained confidence that she was a woman much loved by God, and that made her want to spend more time with the One who created her.

"Now I can go to the mall by myself, venture off on a weekend by myself, go to church and sit by myself, or take a Sunday morning Bible class by myself."

Through discovering who she is before God, Vickie also discovered that she can enjoy life with herself and her God *without* someone physically at her side.

We Discern *Who Our Real Friends Are*

During the times that we walk alone, we discover who our real friends are—who will pray for us, be concerned for us, and still let us be alone when we need to. We all know people who tend to stay away when life gets rough mainly because they don't know what to say or because our pain makes them uncomfortable. A true friend, however, will consider our feelings above her own. And she will also say what needs to be said, not just what we want to hear. Several of my friends who have battled breast cancer testify to the fact that they know who their real friends are today. Lots of people mean well, but it's those who stick with us in the hard times that we know we can count on in future difficulties.

My best friend today is one who proved herself to me during one of my most difficult alone times. I didn't even know her when this book was first published. But over the past eight years this woman has been a rock of support during a difficult time of transition. Through my tears, frustrations, lack of confidence, and even times when I wasn't returning calls or being a good friend to *her*, her love for me never waned. She even boarded a plane and accompanied me to a speaking engagement halfway across the country at her own expense because she knew I would be speaking to leaders and talking about a painful time in my life. She came along, provided prayer support, and made the trip fun for me, showing me that times when people may stay away from us are the times we find out who our *real* friends are.

We Develop *Sensitivity*

We can learn to minister to others who are dealing with similar pain and struggles when we have spent time with God and allowed Him to minister to us. As we discovered earlier from 2 Corinthians 1:3-4, the Lord comforts and ministers to us in our pain and troubles so that we can offer the same comfort to others. Julia recalls that as she experienced the power and compassion and comfort of the Holy Spirit during her alone times with God, she was able to pass on that type of compassion and comfort to others. As we receive from the Lord, He shows us how to give the same to others.

We Get Direction *from God*

Sitting at God's feet helps to clear up our thoughts and enables us to see the truth and get clear direction about the course of our life and the decisions we need to make. It's when we get away from all the other voices in our life and in our world that we can finally hear His voice—and hear what He has to say.[1]

My friend Jini, whom I mentioned in chapters 1 and 10, remembers a time when she was being slandered by a woman in her church who apparently had the reputation of gossiping and attacking others. Jini recalls feeling very alone in this as she tried to garner some support from her husband, the pastor of the church. "I was angry and feeling so misunderstood, and as I was telling my husband about it, he just told me to consider the source and went back to his football game. I literally went into my closet and cried out to God. It was one of those wonderful moments when I sensed the Lord was *there* and I felt He understood my situation perfectly. During that time of pouring out my heart, He filled me with what I believe were His purposes for me in that particular situation. I was alone in my hurt, and yet it afforded me an amazingly intimate time with my Lord."

Have you sensed God's plans and purposes for you in your alone times?

In Oswald Chambers' beloved classic *My Utmost for His Highest*, he asks the question, "Have you ever been alone with God?" Chambers points out that when Jesus was alone with His disciples, that's when He expounded on things, and that's when He shared what was on His heart. Chambers says God wants to do the same with us, but it only happens when we are alone with Him:

> When God gets us alone by affliction, heartbreak, or temptation, by disappointments, sickness, or by thwarted affection, by a broken friendship, or by a new friendship—when he gets us absolutely alone, and we are dumbfounded, and cannot ask one question, then He begins to expound...Jesus can expound nothing until we get through all the noisy questions of the head and are alone with Him.[2]

We Learn the Value of Spiritual Disciplines

Through extended times alone with God, we come to realize the value of prayer, reading God's Word, and other spiritual disciplines. There's the discipline of meditating on God's Word, which involves prayerfully reflecting on Scripture and considering how it applies to our lives. We can also benefit from memorizing God's Word and hiding it in our hearts for the times when we really need it. (So many women I know tell me they can't memorize anything even if their lives depended on it. But anything that we read over and over again will become implanted in our minds. And the more we get alone with God and His Word, the more His Word will be etched in our minds.) Other spiritual disciplines like fasting can become a part of our lives, as well, when we spend time alone with God and relish His presence.

A friend of mine recalls a time in her life when God was tugging at her heart to step down from a high-profile ministry position at her large church. "I felt like I was stepping into death," she said. She knew it was time to go away with God, but she didn't like the feeling of being unproductive, of feeling she had no ministry and "nothing to do." But during those precious years when she wasn't up front ministering to others, she was behind closed doors being ministered to by her Savior. During that season of her life she learned to really pray and fast and memorize and meditate on God's Word. Today she instructs others in the spiritual disciplines, and her life is evidence that she and God have surely "gone away" together.

We Learn to Feel and Think Deeply

Sometimes it doesn't take much effort to feel deeply about something. As women, we are passionate about many things. But to *think* deeply takes time—it's a process of learning to listen to your head and not just your heart (remember that in chapter 8?) and to weigh out options before the Lord. Doing this helps us to slow down and consider the things that we don't take the time to think about when we rush through a quiet time with God or meet with others during a one-hour Bible study. Some of the greatest, most profound think-ers in the Christian faith spent much time alone with God, and the results overflowed from their lives and blessed other people. Wouldn't you like to have such an overflow in your life?

We Will Display Peace

It's no wonder we are told in Psalm 46:10 to "*be still,* and know that I am God" (emphasis added). When we are alone with Him, we get to know Him and we can experience His peace and model it before others. I, personally, am the kind of person who is an absolute wreck if I don't spend time alone with God on a regular basis. Time with Him puts me back in touch with who He is, and when I'm aware of who He is, then I lose my fears and worries and realize that God can take care of *every one* of the things that concern me. Our faith in God is directly related to how well we know God. That old bumper sticker is true: "No God, no peace; know God, know peace."

My friend Barbara tells a touching story of experiencing the peace of God in the depths of depression and feeling very alone. When her sons were 3 years old and 14 months, she was in the worst depression of her life, which only became worse as she faced horrible memories of an abused childhood. One morning after her husband left for work she lay in bed feeling terribly alone, without the strength or willpower to even get out of bed.

"My two little boys got out of bed and my older climbed up on my bed and lay there with me, patting my forehead and gently kissing my cheek. My other son played very contentedly on the floor next to my bed. During those precious moments, Jesus used my children to minister to me, and what a message He spoke to my heart! Such an expression of the sweet love of Jesus!" The Bible tells us that only through God can we get that peace that surpasses understanding (Phi-lippians 4:7), and when we've experienced it, we can display it as well.

We Will Develop Confidence

A woman who depends on God, knows who she is, can discern

who her real friends are, thinks clearly and deeply, and has peace will obviously be a woman who is confident. Our best confidence-building experience in any area of life is, again, getting to know this God who is the author of confidence. Sit before Him and you will experience, firsthand, that you can do "all things through Him who strengthens [you]" (Philippians 4:19).

Hilda learned the truth of that verse through experiencing loss. Hilda, whom I wrote about in chapter 8, who was looking positively at retirement as a time to rest in the Lord, instead found herself widowed shortly into her retirement years. She had been so dependent on her husband while he was living that her grown children and other family members feared she wouldn't be able to make it on her own, living in the woods by herself, handling business matters, paying the bills, and attending to the details of her home that her husband had always taken care of. Yet in her sudden aloneness with just God (because all of her children lived out of state), she says "I felt the greatest peace I had ever known as a Christian. It seemed God spoke to me and said, 'Just trust me...I'm carrying you in My arms. You don't have anything to fear.'"

Hilda continued to live in her home by herself as God provided a renter to occupy her basement and keep her company, provided encouragement from family and friends, and provided her with people and resources to give her clear direction in who to call for whatever situation might occur. Hilda confidently remodeled her home within four months, sold property, and was even able to fly without fear for the first time (and continues today to do so) to visit family members. She even started a widow support group in which she took women on retreats, took them out to eat or celebrate birthdays, and shared with them how to cope in difficult situations. She also provided resources for these women so they would know how to handle legal matters, probate, a will, and so on. Hilda's alone time with God afforded her new opportunities to develop a confidence she would have otherwise never acquired. (Incidentally, a few years after pouring her life into others and encouraging other widows like herself, God unexpectedly brought a new husband into her life.)

Going Away with Him

The benefits we just looked at—all of which come from spending time with God—don't just happen when we cry out to God in the midst of trouble. They come from living alone with God, even when we're surrounded by people. They come from walking through the desert and meeting Him there and finding that a walk with Him during the night is better than a walk without Him during the day.

Jesus is our ultimate example of how to handle life's situations. And Jesus didn't just go to His Father when He saw trouble coming on. He didn't go away with God only when no one else was around. He regularly sought out times to be alone with the Father. Jesus, being God in the flesh, had no one on this earth who could relate to what He experienced when He lived here among men. So He looked forward to being with the One who knew Him better than any other and the only One who could refresh Him.

In Scripture we're told that when the crowds pressed in on Jesus, He would withdraw to a quiet place where He could be alone. I don't think it was because He was weary of being around people and their endless demands. I think it was because He felt God tugging at His heart and saying, "Come away with Me, My Son, let's spend some time together—alone." And Jesus responded. He knew He needed that. And I believe, during that time when He was alone with God, there was no other place He wanted to be.

When Jesus was alone with God, His Father, I imagine the two shared each other's hearts. Jesus told His Father what was on His heart, and God revealed to His Son the same. We know from Jesus' prayer in John 17 that God revealed His will to Jesus, and Jesus followed through. That kind of fellowship and oneness came through their alone times together. And during that prayer, one of Jesus' last prayers before leaving this earth, Jesus revealed His desire for *our* relationship with God. His desire was that we be one with Him, just as

Jesus and God are one with each other. Jesus prayed, "I have given them the glory that you gave me, that they may be one as we are one: I in them and you in me. May they be brought to *complete unity* to let the world know that you sent me and have *loved them even as you have loved me"* (verses 22-23, emphasis added).

I believe Jesus was praying that you and I would one day know the kind of intimacy with Him that He had with His Father. Think of it…to be able to have a oneness and unity with Christ that is like that which Christ shared with God. That is an incredible thought! And it is an incredible possibility because it is something Jesus specifically prayed for *us*.

Do you want to know Him in that way? I do. Imagine the peace, the rest, the joy of being one with the living God…of experiencing His love, His comfort, His strength, His power. What a way to live! When we are alone, we are one with Him. When we awake in the morning, we are one with Him. When we lie down to sleep at the end of the day, our heart is one with Him. Oh, to experience that oneness! To be able to say to God, as Jesus did in that same prayer, "All I have is yours, and all you have is mine" (verse 10).

Getting to that Place

So how do we do it? Jesus was one with God because He took time to sit at God's feet. He took time to pray, time to be alone with His Father.

After a whirlwind eight months of moving to a new city, settling into a new home, taking a new position in a church, transitioning my daughter to a new school and neighborhood, teaching Bible studies and classes, meeting a demanding speaking schedule, and writing this book, I came to see that what I needed in my life was not something more to do, not something to make me feel significant, not something to make me feel I'm doing more for God. What I needed was more of *God*. And ever since I made this move, God has been impressing on my heart that He is not impressed with my busyness, but with the amount of time I am willing to sit at His feet, completely absorbed in Him. He wants me to spend less time in *activity* for Him and more time *alone* with Him.[3]

Now, that's difficult these days. The world we live in—and even the churches we attend—are not favorable to the whole idea of "doing less and sitting more"—especially when there's nothing to show for it. You see, no one can measure our "success" by the time we spend alone with God. And it's not something that pays monetarily or produces something visually or stands out on a resume or adds to our list of ministry experience or puts extra letters after our name. But it's something that conforms our character, blesses us internally, and develops us into the people God designed us to be.

So how, exactly, do we go live the adventure of being alone with our God? From Scripture I find that we must:

- *Sit at His feet.* This means basking in His presence, worshipping Him (like we talked about in chapter 6), getting quiet enough to hear Him speak to our hearts. It means letting the world rush by while we rest in Him.

  In Mark 1:35, we read about how one time, Jesus rose early in the morning while it was still dark and "went off to a solitary place, where he prayed." When His followers found out He was gone, they had a fit! They all went looking for Him, and when they found Him they said, basically, "What do You think you're doing? Everyone's looking for You. You have a job to do!"

  When you, too, seek out a lonely place like Jesus did, chances are other people won't like to see you go. They'll want to give you something more to do, or be your special friend, or find you a date, or take you to the mall…anything but let you be alone. They mean well, of course, just as Jesus' friends meant well. But it's vital that we not let anything encroach upon our time alone with God.

- *Soak in His Word.* When you spend time in God's Word, don't just read it. Swim in it, soak in it a while, and get so deep into it that you find yourself drowning in it. I like to start in the Psalms, songs of such human emotion, and paraphrase them, making them personal songs of praise to Jesus. Then I'll spend time in study of some other portion of Scripture.

Another meaningful exercise is to go through the Gospels (Matthew, Mark, Luke, and John), reading about Jesus and closing your eyes and putting yourself in the scene. Ask yourself: What would I have said or how would I have felt if Jesus had said those words to me or touched me with His outstretched hand? Experience the stories by being there in your mind and heart. The Bible will come alive for you like it never has before!

- *Seek His will.* What does God want for your life? The only way you can know is by spending time with Him and with His Word. In the Bible, God tells us a lot about how He desires for us to live. And when we pray, we can ask Him to help us view our lives, circumstances, and opportunities the same way that He views them. It's when we gain His perspective on things that we're more sensitive to His leading in our lives.

As you seek to do God's will at all times, you'll find great fulfillment, for then you'll be living out His purpose in your life. And there's *nothing* you can do that's greater than that!

Entering the Arena of Abundance

My friend, as you take your alone times and funnel them into opportunities to sit at His feet, soak in His Word, and seek His will, you cannot help but be strengthened from the inside out. You cannot help but find His Oasis in your desert and drink of his Living Water that will satisfy your soul.

That Oasis of Living Water waits for you—so come, drink, and live! And then reach out to a woman who is weary of walking alone and lead her to the place of abundance by Jesus' side, where she, too, can find strength and hope.

Remember, Jesus said *all* that He has is ours—*all* of His comfort, *all* of His love, *all* of His power, *all* of His strength—for any season of our life.

I want to experience it. Don't *you?*

Entering the Oasis

For Personal Application

1. Which of the benefits on pages 195-202 have you personally experienced during the course of this study?

2. Jesus said to His followers in Mark 6:31, "Come with me by yourselves to a quiet place and get some rest." Where is your quiet place where you can "go away" with Jesus? It might be a place you drive to, or your living room chair when the house is quiet. Schedule a time and place to go there soon. Bring your Bible, a journal if you wish, and spend some quiet time letting Him speak to your heart through His Word. Record your thoughts, prayers, or specific verses that God may be speaking to your heart.

3. If you'd like to apply this concept of "going away with God in your heart" on a regular basis, you can do so by beginning a study (with a friend or on your own) of my book *When Women Long for Rest: God's Peace for Your Overwhelmed Life.*

For Further Study

Read Psalm 23 slowly. Notice the ways God ministers to us when we are alone with Him. Write out each way that our Shepherd is an oasis of refreshment to us when we are weary and thirsty like sheep on a long journey.

Prayerfully reflect on the following verses and indicate next to each reference how God is an oasis in your life.

Psalm 63:1-8:

Psalm 65:9-13:

Isaiah 58:11:

Jeremiah 17:7-8:

Read Psalm 62 and list at least five reasons for waiting on God alone:

Thank God for where He has met you in this study and ask Him to open the door to where He wants you to go and how He wants you to grow from here.

Welcome to the Oasis

ou made it, my friend! You walked through those deserts of life that often keep us from growing and you've found your source of strength. Remember, there is no place you can walk where God will not go with you. And there is no place you can fall where He cannot pick you up. And there is no thirst in your life that His living water cannot satisfy.

Remain close to His Oasis and be strengthened knowing that whatever the season of life, because of Jesus, you will never walk alone!

Appendix
SURRENDERING THE STRUGGLE

Surrendering the struggle against loneliness first involves surrendering to God—in every way. God, being holy and without sin, demands that we surrender our lives to Him by repenting of our sin and accepting His Son as our means to forgiveness and righteousness. Whether or not our sin has caused our state of aloneness, we are still people with a sin problem (Romans 3:23), and it manifests itself in our pride that wants to live our lives how *we* want rather than how our Maker wants. Before we can give our loneliness problem to God and have Him meet us there, we must give to Him our sin problem so He can put us in the position where He can help us.

To surrender to God, we must:

1. Admit we are sinners by nature and there is nothing we can do on our own to make up for that sin in the eyes of a holy God.

2. Accept the sacrifice that God provided—the death of His sinless Son, Jesus, on the cross on our behalf—in order to bring us into communion with Him.

3. Enter into a love relationship with God, through Jesus, as a response to His love and forgiveness toward you.

(For more on developing and maintaining an intimate relationship with God, see my book *Letting God Meet Your Emotional Needs* by Harvest House Publishers.)

4. Surrender to God your right to yourself and acknowledge His right to carry out His plans for you and to mold you, shape you, and transform you for His pleasure.

5. Find a pastor or women's ministry director at a Bible-believing church in your area or a trusted Christian friend and tell him or her of your decision to surrender your life to Christ. They will want to pray for you and get you the support you need to grow in your new relationship with Jesus.

Small Group
Leader's Guide

༄

Dear Study Group Facilitator:

Your desire to lead a small group through this book thrills my heart. I have written the following lesson plans so you can go through this study in 11 or 12 weeks—covering the introduction and chapter 1 the first week, and then one chapter a week for the remaining 10 weeks (or you can cover only the introduction the first week and then do chapter 1 during the second week and continuing one chapter a week thereafter). In my experience, I have seen less drop-off in attendance when women's studies are 12 weeks or less. However, you know your group of women best. This is your study, so adapt as you feel will best accommodate your participants.

The aim of each session is for the women to connect with one another and feel safe enough that they can be transparent with one another so they are encouraged and strengthened in their walk with God.

May the Lord bless you as you walk alongside the women in your group and encourage them with the truth that as God's children, they never truly walk alone.

In His unfailing love,
Cindi McMenamin

Preparing to Start the Group

1. Pray in advance about which women would benefit from a study of this book.

2. Send out handwritten or email invitations or make personal phone calls and invite these women to come together and meet as a group.

3. Continue to pray for each woman whom you have invited to be a part of the group.

4. Make available to each participant a copy of the book. Have the women read a chapter each week and encourage them to come prepared to discuss that week's chapter.

5. Print out a schedule with the dates you meet and the chapters to be studied. This will help participants to stay on track in case they miss a week or two.

6. It is most helpful for the facilitator to have read the entire book (and answered all of the application questions) before starting the group study. This way the leader knows what's coming and can keep each meeting's discussion on topic. It will also let the leader know what is coming up in the future, in case questions arise that are better answered in future meetings).

Introduction: A Cry from the Desert

Welcome the women to the study. Introduce yourself as their facilitator. Have each woman introduce herself and tell why she desires to study *When Women Walk Alone*.

Tell the group how you can relate, personally, to this subject matter. Share with them what you hope to get out of the study, as well as your goal for the women in the group.

Open the study session in prayer.

If the group hasn't read the introduction yet, read it out loud (or pick a few women who can take turns reading it out loud).

1. Look at the table of contents and note that the book is divided into three sections. Look at the chapters in each section. Which season of life do you find yourself in right now?

2. Read through the bullet points on pages 14-15. These are the "stressors" that cause the author to feel alone. Which can you relate to, and what could you add to that list?

   Read out loud the first paragraph below the bullet points on page 15.

   This is the goal of this study—that we each learn to see our alone times as invitations to be alone with God and see a new side of Him. Our prayer is that our times in the desert will serve as opportunities to enter into a deeper relationship with God.

   We're going to delve chapter by chapter into the main areas of aloneness for women.

3. Commit to praying for each other throughout this study. You may want to assign prayer partners for this study, or have each woman voluntarily team up with another to pray with her and hold her accountable through the next 10-12 weeks.

Assignment: Have the women read chapter 1 during the next week (or have them read chapter 2 if you already decided to cover chapter 1 in your first meeting).

Close your time together in prayer.

Chapter 1: Alone as a Woman

....

Key Point: Embrace your alone times because they present to you an opportunity to grow closer to God.

Opening Discussion Question: What portions did you highlight, or what really stood out to you in this chapter?

....

1. Did you notice the key to Julia's turnaround on page 20?

   She soon discovered that her identity was not wrapped up in her circumstances—that is, who she was married to and what was expected of her—but rather, in who she was before a God who loved her.

2. Turn to page 211 and emphasize the importance of "Surrendering the Struggle" at the outset of the study so the participants can truly understand and grow through this study. Give the women an opportunity to go through these steps if they haven't already, or extend the invitation to them to talk to you privately with any questions they have about receiving God's gift of eternal life and entering into a personal relationship with Christ.

3. Ask the women which of the scenarios on pages 21-23 they can most relate to.

4. On pages 25-26, we looked at "Counting the Blessings." The author's struggle was secondary infertility. What have you felt that God is withholding from you in your life?

5. Share your list of the "good things" in your life right now. Which of these would you not have today if you had all that you were hoping God would give you?

6. Take to God that area of aloneness that you struggle with and surrender it to Him, asking Him to show you the blessings that lie therein. You can do this by completing the next exercise.

7. Read the following verses and list the ways God intends to bless you.

- Jeremiah 29:11
- Psalm 37:4
- Romans 8:28-30

Using these verses as a guide, pray God's will, not yours, in your area of struggles or aloneness.

8. Who can you share with this week about your experience in the alone times and where God met you?

Assignment: Have the women read chapter 2 and work through the application questions for next week. Encourage them to highlight any portions of the reading that stood out or impacted them in a particular way or that they'd like to discuss in the group.

Chapter 2: Alone at Heart

Key Point: God is the perfect "husband," whether you have one or not.

Opening Discussion Question: What portions of the book did you highlight, or what really stood out to you in this chapter?

Review the first paragraph of the section "No One to Help" on page 33. Can you relate to what is stated in this paragraph?

Read Leah's story in Genesis 29:14-35.

1. In what area of your life do you need to finally say (as Leah did), "*This time* I will praise the Lord"?

2. Read Isaiah 54:5. What does it really mean to see the Lord as our "husband"?

3. Review the steps on pages 40-42, and discuss practical ways to incorporate each step.

4. Continue with the exercises on pages 43-46.

Assignment: Have the women read chapter 3 and work through the application questions for next week. Encourage them to highlight any portions of the reading that stood out or impacted them in a particular way or that they'd like to discuss in the group.

Chapter 3: Alone as a Parent

....

Key Point: God cares about your child even more than you do, so partner with Him in your prayers, concerns, and parenting.

Opening Discussion Question: In what ways do you feel alone as you parent your child or children?

....

This chapter points out that the role of parenting was never meant for one person alone. Yet there are a surprisingly high number of single parents raising children today. Though God never meant for you to parent alone, He stands ready to help you, regardless of your situation.

1. Desiree, in her story, listed some hidden blessings of single parenting. What blessings come to your mind as you think of the "alone times" in parenting?

2. Review the elements of "God's Provision for the Single Parent" on pages 52-57.

3. Review the Personal Application and For Further Study questions on pages 58-60.

Have the women pair up and spend some time in prayer for each other as mothers, lifting up the concerns for each other's children before the Lord.

Assignment: Have the women read chapter 4 and work through the application questions for next week. Encourage them to highlight any

portions of the reading that stood out or impacted them i
way or that they'd like to discuss in the group.

Chapter 4: Alone in Your P~~igh~~ which we

ve open that door

Key Point: Our hidden pain can be the do
discover a deeper love and forgiveness fr~~o~~
and allow Him in.   of this chapter impacted

Opening Discussion Question: Whi
you the most?

~~e~~ group.

Read Psalm 40:1-3 ou~~r~~ou~~

~~nen can relate to being in a "slimy pit"

1. Ask i~~f~~ any of t~~h~~~~od~~ pulling them from the mud and mire.
   or experienci~~
~~s God heals our pain (see pages 70-72) by:
2. Review the~~

   • Light~~in~~g our load
   • Lig~~ht~~ng up our life with hope
   • L~~ift~~ing our heads

3. ~~As~~k the women which of the above three healing touches
   ~~t~~hey need from God right now.
4. On pages 72-75 are listed five steps for gaining
   perspective in the midst of our pain. Which of these
   is most challenging? Have the women share their
   observations and insights.
5. Review the Personal Application and For Further Study
   questions on pages 76-77.

Spend some time praying for the women in your group. You may want
to offer up a prayer for any hurts that might not have been discussed

it all and

ye the women, through prayer, that God knows
Assignmer to heal them completely and unconditionally.
application ques.
tions of the reading women read chapter 5 and work through the
or that they'd like to a. week. Encourage them to highlight any por-
ut or impacted them in a particular way

group.

Chapter 5: An

.... our Spiritual Life

Key Point: Feeling alone spiritually ....
upon and trust in God.   d us to a greater dependence

Opening Discussion Question: In what w
tually, whether or not your husband is a be you felt alone spiri-
.... ?

1. Summarize the "Wisdom for Wives" on p. 86-90.
   Ask the women which of these five points w d be most
   helpful to them and their husband right now.

2. Talk about the concept of "releasing and trusting
   well as the idea that "any heart can change." Ask t
   women if they are in a place of releasing and trustin and
   continuing to believe that only God—and not their o n
   efforts—can bring about true change in someone's hea.

Review the Personal Application and For Further Study questions on pages 95-97.

End the session by sharing practical ways that the unmarried women
in the group can look to God for their spiritual encouragement, and
the married women can focus on encouraging their husband, regardless of his spiritual condition. Make these things a matter of prayer
with the group.

Assignment: Have the women read chapter 6 and work through the application questions for next week. Encourage them to highlight any portions of the reading that stood out or impacted them in a particular way or that they'd like to discuss in the group.

If possible, schedule a little longer for next week's lesson on worship so you can do some creative things with the women so they actually engage in worship during your time together, instead of just talking about it.

Chapter 6: Alone in Worship

Key Point: Worship is a very personal thing. See it as something you can enjoy with God alone.

Opening Discussion Question: Describe a time when you have experienced very meaningful worship which blessed your heart.

1. Review the first Personal Application question on page 113. Have the women share what they did to spend time alone with the Lord.

2. Play a worship song that the women can reflect on, and listen to the words. (A favorite of mine is Matthew Ward's "I Will Worship You" on his *Even Now* CD, which is available on YouTube.com. I have women write down the one-word descriptions that Matthew sings throughout the song that describe who God is. It's very powerful!)

3. Ask if anyone took a "worship walk" this past week and if so, ask if they'd like to share what happened during that time. If time and location permit, have the women get up and take a worship walk through the neighborhood outside or wherever you are meeting. Audibly praise God for everything you see and hear and feel and anything that comes to your mind during this walk.

4. Ask if anyone would like to share the names they came up with for God in response to question 3 on page 114.

Lead the women in that exercise and come up with
some names together. This is one of the easiest and most
effective ways we can worship the Lord.

5. Ask if anyone would like to share their goals for how they
can worship God more.

6. Have the women read out loud the verses listed in the For
Further Study section, and have them share their one-
sentence responses for each verse as it's read, if they feel
comfortable doing so.

Close the session in prayer, asking God to help each of you worship
Him more often during the week and as a way of life.

*Assignment: Have the women read chapter 7 and work through
the application questions for next week. Encourage them to highlight
any portions of the reading that stood out or impacted them in a particular way or that they'd like to discuss in the group.*

Chapter 7: Alone in Your Trials

....

Key Point: God is writing your glory story amid the troubles and trials you see in your life right now. Don't let them be for nothing. Surrender and let Him turn your suffering into a song that praises Him.

Opening Discussion Question: When you think of testing and trials in
your life, what comes to mind right now? (If you can't think of any,
make this a point of praise to God. If you can think of some, this lesson will help you turn your trials into points of praise.)

....

1. Summarize the ways trials help develop our strength (see
pages 125-127). Which of these benefits do you see God
working into your life right now?

2. Review the Personal Application questions at the end of
the chapter.

3. In the For Further Study section, read out loud the portions of Scripture in Job that are listed with each question (and choose some passages ahead of time in chapters 38–41) in case anyone in your group is unfamiliar with the biblical account of Job or did not read the chapter or the portions of Scripture. Don't shy away from including too much Scripture in retelling this story. That is where the power resides in this lesson!

Close your time together by praising God for the glory story He is writing in each of your lives.

Assignment: Have the women read chapter 8 and work through the application questions for next week. Encourage them to highlight any portions of the reading that stood out or impacted them in a particular way or that they'd like to discuss in the group.

Chapter 8: Alone in Your Restlessness

Key Point: Our restlessness can drive us to a deeper desperation for God if we take our frustrations to Him.

Opening Discussion Question: Can you relate to a season of restlessness in your life? If so, what do you feel desperate or restless for?

Review the "Putting It into Practice" steps on pages 146-150. Ask the women which of these steps they most need to put into practice right now.

Lead the women through the Personal Application and For Further Study questions on pages 152-154. Be prepared to stop the lesson and pray for certain women as issues come up that they are feeling restless about. Discuss the importance of accountability to one another and your mutual desire to see each other avoid falling into traps we may face when we feel desperate or restless. Bathe this study in prayer, before and after, and follow up with the women during the week, if needed.

Close the session together in prayer.

Assignment: Have the women read chapter 9 and work through the application questions for next week. Encourage them to highlight any portions of the reading that stood out or impacted them in a particular way or that they'd like to discuss in the group.

Chapter 9: Alone in Your Dreams

Key Point: God wants to do through you what is beyond you, and He is often the only One who can make it happen.

Opening Discussion Question: What have you always wanted to do but haven't felt supported or qualified to do it? (Listen to and encourage the women as they share their dreams. This can be a beneficial time of healing and encouragement as they share openly about something they've always longed to do.)

Review pages 162-166 and consider the steps that Esther followed. Ask the women which one of these steps they need to focus on right now:

Consider her calling?

Gather prayer support?

Make a plan and carry it out?

Trust in the unseen?

Go through the Personal Application and For Further Study questions at the end of the chapter. Have the women pray in pairs for each other's dreams and specific calling.

Assignment: Have the women read chapter 10 and work through the application questions for next week. Encourage them to highlight any portions of the reading that stood out or impacted them in a particular way or that they'd like to discuss in the group.

Chapter 10: Alone in Serving

....

Key Point: Our frustrations and alone times that come when serving others make us more like Jesus and help us relate to His heart.

Opening Discussion Question: Have you ever felt alone or frustrated as you've stepped out to serve others? What made you feel that way?

....

1. Lead women through the Personal Application questions at the end of this chapter.

2. As you go through the For Further Study section, read the entire passage from John 15 out loud, then review the answers line by line. Talk about the concept of pruning (and the types of situations that would bring about pruning or refine us and cause us to grow) when we're serving and obeying Christ.

3. Pray for the women as they continue to serve, or as they consider stepping back into service, or as they search for a place in their church where they can serve. Remember, serving isn't always done in an official capacity. Ministry happens every day as we look for divine appointments and respond obediently to where God would have us reach out, encourage, serve, or sacrifice.

Assignment: Have the women read chapter 11 and work through the application questions for next week. Encourage them to highlight any portions of the reading that stood out or impacted them in a particular way or that they'd like to discuss in the group.

Chapter 11: Alone with Your God

....

Key Point: We can go from the desert of our aloneness to the oasis of abundance when we long to be with God—alone.

Opening Discussion Question: What impacted you the most in this chapter, or in this entire study?

....

1. Review the benefits of being alone (given on pages 195-202). Ask the women which ones they have experienced while going through this study.

2. Encourage the women to think of or talk about their quiet place, where they go to be with God alone. Talk about what they can do during their time with God. Now might be a good time to talk about what study everyone wants to do next. Depending on everyone's interest level, consider a study of *When Women Long for Rest*, or *When a Woman Discovers Her Dream*.

3. Lead the women through the For Further Study questions, reading the scriptures out loud and getting their observations and insights.

Read "Welcome to the Oasis" (page 209) and close the study in prayer, asking God to keep the women desperate for Him.

If you desire to do so, you can direct the women to the last page of this book—"An Invitation to Write"—and encourage them to contact me with their comments about the study group and how it impacted their life. I would love to hear from each one of them.

God's blessings on you, dear friend,
for leading others through this study.

Notes

Chapter 2—Alone at Heart

1. For more on this concept, see chapter one of my book *Letting God Meet Your Emotional Needs* (Eugene, OR: Harvest House Publishers, 2003).

2. Zephaniah 3:17 says that God takes "great delight in you, he will quiet you with his love, he will rejoice over you with singing."

Chapter 3—Alone as a Parent

1. This story is found in Genesis 16:1-15.

2. Hebrews 11:6 says, "Without faith it is impossible to please God, because anyone who comes to him must believe that he exists and that he rewards those who earnestly seek him."

3. Philippians 4:19 says, "My God will meet all your needs according to his glorious riches in Christ Jesus."

4. Hebrews 4:15-16 says, "We do not have a high priest who is unable to sympathize with our weaknesses, but we have one who has been tempted in every way, just as we are—yet was without sin. Let us then approach the throne of grace with confidence, so that we may receive mercy and find grace to help us in our time of need."

5. Bible scholars believe Joseph died somewhere between Jesus' twelfth year and adulthood because Joseph is no longer mentioned after Jesus' trip to Jerusalem with his parents when he was 12. Another passage that supports this is John 19:25-27, in which Jesus assigns John to care for his mother after his death. In all likelihood, Joseph would have done this if he had still been around.

6. Lewis Sperry Chafer, *He That Is Spiritual* (Grand Rapids: Zondervan, 1967), p. 32.

Chapter 4—Alone in Your Pain

1. This story is found in Luke 7:36-50.

2. *Beauty Restored: Finding Life and Hope After Date Rape* by Me Ra Koh is available in limited quantities on Amazon.com.

3. To order an audiotape of Dr. John MacArthur's message "The Ministry of Reconciliation" delivered

at the 1999 Harvest Crusade's "Preach the Word" Conference, call 1-800-821-3300, or order online at www.preachtheword.org.

4. Second Corinthians 1:3-4 says that God "comforts us in all our troubles, so that we can comfort those in any trouble with the comfort we ourselves have received from God."

5. Me Ra Koh, *Beauty Restored* (Ventura, CA: Regal Books, 2001), p. 94.

6. Ibid., p. 95.

7. Philippians 4:8 tells us "whatever is true, whatever is noble, whatever is right, whatever is pure, whatever is lovely, whatever is admirable—if anything is excellent or praiseworthy—think about such things."

8. Elizabeth George, *Loving God with All Your Mind* (Eugene, OR: Harvest House, 1994), p. 14.

Chapter 5—Alone in Your Spiritual Life

1. This story is found in Judges 4:1-16

2. This story is found in Exodus 2:1-10.

3. First Samuel 25:1-42.

4. Barna Research Online can be accessed at www.barna.org. The statistics listed in this chapter are from a national survey of Americans conducted in the year 2000.

5. Forty-six percent of women have accepted Christ as their Savior, compared to 36 percent of men.

6. The study showed 45 percent of women attend church on a given Sunday, as opposed to 35 percent of men.

7. The study showed that 45 percent of women had read their Bible in the past week, compared to 35 percent of men who reported reading their Bible in the past week. Also, 22 percent of the women said they regularly attended a Sunday school class (compared to 14 percent of men) and 20 percent of women participated in a small group (compared to 13 percent of men).

8. Eighty-nine percent of women reported praying in the past week, compared to 77 percent of men.

9. Charles R. Swindoll, *Esther: A Woman of Strength and Dignity* (Nashville, TN: Word Publishing, 1997), p. 53.

10. In Mark 10:9, Jesus said, "Therefore what God has joined together, let man not separate." Two verses later, Jesus said, "Anyone who divorces his wife and marries another woman commits adultery against her. And if she divorces her husband and marries another man, she commits adultery."

11. The apostle Paul gave this instruction in 1 Corinthians 7:13: "If a woman has a husband who is not a believer and he is willing to live with her, she must not divorce him."

12. Darien B. Cooper, *You Can Be the Wife of a Happy Husband* (Wheaton, IL: Victor Books, 1974).

13. Jennifer's biblical instruction is found primarily in 1 Corinthians 7:10-11, 13-17.

Chapter 6—Alone in Worship

1. Henry T. Blackaby, *Created to Be God's Friend* (Nashville, TN: Thomas Nelson Publishers, 1999), p. 83.

2. Ibid., p. 83.

3. In Matthew 6:26, Jesus said to His followers, "Look at the birds of the air; they do not sow or reap or store away in barns, and yet your heavenly Father feeds them. Are you not much more valuable than they?"

Chapter 7—Alone in Your Trials

1. This story is found in the book of Ruth.

2. The details of Paul's suffering are found in 2 Corinthians 11:23-27.

Chapter 8—Alone in Your Restlessness

1. Proverbs 14:12; 16:25.

2. Genesis 3:1-19.

3. Genesis 16:1-12.

4. Genesis 30:22-24.

5. David's affair with Bathsheba (detailed in 2 Samuel 11–12:25) resulted in the death of Bathsheba's husband, Uriah, the death of David and Bathsheba's newborn child, and the death, temporarily, of an intimacy with God that David had previously experienced. David's disobedience to God by taking a census of Israel's troops (see 2 Samuel 24:1-15) resulted in the death of 70,000 Israelites.

6. Christi is also the author of *The Blessings of Barrenness: How to Surrender Infertility and Pregnancy Loss.* For more information about her book and ministry, see www.ChristiKari.com.

Chapter 10—Alone in Serving

1. For more information on SMORE, see www.smoreforwomen.org or contact Gail Showalter at singlemoms@smoreforwomen.org. Her blog can be found at smoreforwomen.wordpress.com.

2. Oswald Chambers, *My Utmost for His Highest,* rev. ed. ed. James Reimann (Grand Rapids, MI: Discovery House, 1992), April 22.

3. This section first appeared in the chapter "Keep At It" in Cindi McMenamin's book *When You're Running on Empty* (Eugene, OR: Harvest House, 2006).

Chapter 11—Alone with Your God

1. For more on listening to God, see the chapter "Listening to His Loving Voice" in my book *Letting God Meet Your Emotional Needs* (Eugene, OR: Harvest House Publishers, 2003).

2. Oswald Chambers, *My Utmost for His Highest* (Westwood, NJ: Barbour and Co., 1935, 1963), pp. 9-10.

3. I expanded on this concept a year later in my book *When Women Long for Rest* (Eugene, OR: Harvest House, 2004).

Other Harvest House Books
by Cindi McMenamin

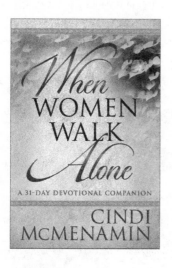

WHEN WOMEN WALK ALONE: A 31-DAY DEVOTIONAL COMPANION

God is at your side, ready to speak to your heart. He knows your every need, whether it be for guidance, encouragement, or comfort. Discover what it means to experience God's presence at all times with the help of this 31-day devotional companion. And face each day with a renewed sense of hope and fulfillment that comes from resting in God's love. Can be used alone or as a companion volume to *When Women Walk Alone*.

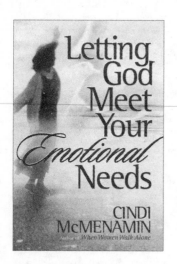

LETTING GOD MEET YOUR EMOTIONAL NEEDS

Do you long to have your emotional needs met, yet find that your husband or those close to you cannot always help bring fulfillment to your life? Discover true intimacy with God in this book that shows how to draw closer to the lover of your soul and find that He can, indeed, meet your deepest emotional needs.

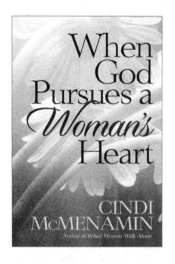

WHEN GOD PURSUES A WOMAN'S HEART

Within the heart of every woman is the desire to be cherished and loved. Recapture the romance of a relationship with God as you discover the many ways God loves you and pursues your heart as your Hero, Provider, Comforter, Friend, Valiant Knight, Loving Daddy, Perfect Prince, and more.

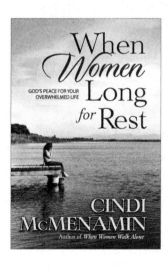

WHEN WOMEN LONG FOR REST

Women today are tired of feeling overwhelmed by all the demands on their lives and are longing for rest. They want to do more than just simplify or reorganize their lives. *When Women Long for Rest* is an invitation for women to find their quiet place at God's feet—a place where they can listen to Him, open their hearts to Him, and experience true rest.

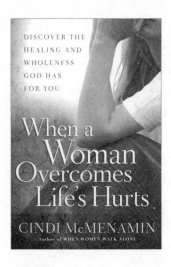

When a Woman Overcomes Life's Hurts

Only God can take the bitter things and turn them into blessings in your own life and the lives of others. Cindi shares powerful examples of the ways God has changed broken lives, offering encouraging counsel that will lead you toward a renewed focus on God, a resurgence of inner joy, and better relationships with others.

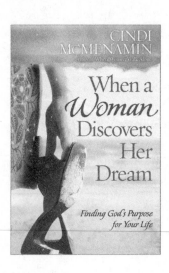

When a Woman Discovers Her Dream

When it comes to living out the dream God has placed on your heart, do you shrug your shoulders and say, "It's too late…it's too far out of reach…it's too impossible for someone like me"? But you *can* live out that dream—no matter what your stage or place in life. Join Cindi as she shares how you can explore God's purposes for your life, make greater use of your special gifts, turn your dreams into reality, and become the masterpiece God designed you to be.

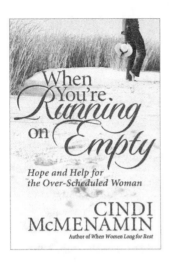

WHEN YOU'RE RUNNING ON EMPTY

Are you feeling run down and ready to give up? If so, then you're probably running on empty. And you may feel as if the pressures and stress will never end. But there is a way out. Cindi shares from her own life and struggles many helpful and practical secrets about simplifying your priorities and obligations, rejuvenating yourself through God's Word, cultivating health habits that renew your energy, and learning to please God and not people.

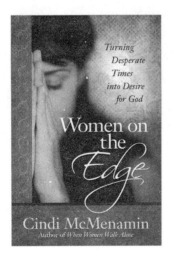

WOMEN ON THE EDGE

We all have times when we find ourselves on the verge of frustration, despair, or even a meltdown. And we find ourselves at a crossroads: One path cries out for us to escape it all. The other calls us to persevere and lean on the Lord. Rather than merely survive, choose to abundantly thrive—by learning how to yield all control of your life to God, rest in His purpose and plan for your life, and enjoy the confidence of a heart wholly surrendered to Him.

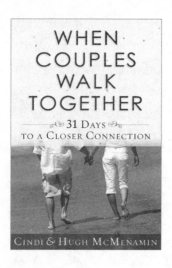

When Couples Walk Together
(with Hugh McMenamin)

Are the demands of everyday life constantly pulling you and your spouse in different directions? If you've longed to rekindle the intimacy and companionship that first brought you together, join Hugh and Cindi McMenamin as they share 31 days of simple, creative, and fun ways you can draw closer together again. You'll find your marriage greatly enriched as you experience anew the joys of togetherness and unselfish love.

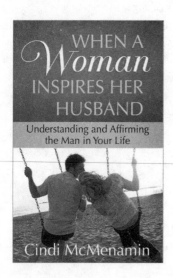

When a Woman Inspires Her Husband

Discover how you can be the encourager, motivator, inspiration, and admiration behind your husband—the wind beneath his wings—as you understand his world, become his cheerleader, appreciate his differences, ease his burdens, and encourage him to dream. An uplifting resource designed to strengthen your marriage.

An Invitation to Write

Where has God met you on your journey of aloneness? If you would like to share with Cindi how God has used *When Women Walk Alone* in your life, she would love to hear from you.

You can contact Cindi online at
Cindi@StrengthForTheSoul.com or write:

Cindi McMenamin
c/o Harvest House Publishers
990 Owen Loop North
Eugene, OR 97402-9173

You can also find Cindi on Facebook at
Strength for the Soul.

If you would like to have Cindi speak to your group, you can find more information about her speaking ministry at www.StrengthForTheSoul.com.

To learn more about Harvest House books and
to read sample chapters, log on to our website:

www.harvesthousepublishers.com

HARVEST HOUSE PUBLISHERS
EUGENE, OREGON